Sandra,

Love and all good wishes
at Christmas and for
the New Year. 1993,

from

Reg: and William

English
PRIVATE
GARDENS

English PRIVATE GARDENS

**OPEN TO THE PUBLIC IN AID OF THE
NATIONAL GARDENS SCHEME**

*Judy Johnson and Susan Berry
Photography by Steven Wooster*

Foreword by Beth Chatto

COLLINS & BROWN

First published in Great Britain in 1991
by Collins & Brown Limited
Mercury House
195 Knightsbridge
London SW7 1RE

A CIP catalogue record for this book
is available from the British Library

ISBN 1 85585 041 9

Conceived, edited and designed by Collins & Brown Limited

Editorial Director **Gabrielle Townsend**

Editors **Penny David & Sarah Bloxham**

Art Director **Roger Bristow**

Designer **Steven Wooster**

Filmset by Tradespools Ltd, Frome, Somerset

Reproduction by Scantrans, Singapore

Printed and bound in Italy by New Interlitho, SpA, Milan

Contents

Foreword

I T IS A PRIVILEGE to own a patch of land however small; to be able to make a live, constantly changing picture; to dig and dream to one's heart's content, whether it be a whole commitment, or a small part of oneself set aside from the rest of life's responsibilities. To make a garden can prove to be a life-enhancing therapy, despite frustrations and hazards such as pests and diseases, climatic extremes, or more mundane things like bad backs and ragged finger nails. Unlike more finite forms of art, the end result can far exceed the small efforts we make to begin the magical progression of a garden. We may plot and plan, take cuttings, sow seeds, cosset the soil, but then the plants take over, filling the empty spaces, not only at ground level but lifting our eyes and spirits to where, given time, they will reach up and touch the sky.

As students of painting and fine art visit galleries, great houses and museums for direction and inspiration, so gardeners love to visit other gardens to talk with gardeners, discover new plants, discuss what to do with them, and sometimes be bowled over by a totally unexpected combination.

I was fortunate during the formative years of my gardening life to have the friendship of a great artist-gardener, Sir Cedric Morris, of Hadleigh, Suffolk. Both he and his garden are no more, but Cedric's plants flourish still in many hundreds of gardens made by his visitors, while his ideas are scattered like seeds, sown into our consciousness. His was not a conventional garden based on formal or premeditated design. Looking back I feel it was an extension of his palette with colours and shapes emerging spontaneously and dissolving like flowers scattered through an alpine meadow, yet it would never have qualified for today's definition of a meadow garden.

Gardens opened under the National Gardens Scheme can be found in all sizes; neither age nor fame is a prerequisite. In some

The early autumn light, right, brings out the soft golden and russet tones of the marginal plants in Beth Chatto's water garden.

Beth Chatto in her Mediterranean garden, right, among closely packed drought-resistant plants.

villages an enchanting afternoon can be spent wandering in and out of several small gardens, each individual and likely to offer accessible ideas. Sometimes one learns by seeing examples of what not to do or, perhaps more fairly, sees what would not be suitable in one's own garden.

Many beautiful gardens open to the public today are available because their owners have been encouraged by the National Gardens Scheme Charitable Trust. This organization started in 1927 as a one-off event to raise money for a memorial to Queen Alexandra. Miss Elsie Wagg, a council member of the Queen's Nursing Institute, which funded, trained and set the standards of District Nursing, said that it was a shame that the only people presently enjoying the many outstanding privately owned gardens were the owners themselves and their friends; they should open to the public for one day to share their beauty while also raising funds for the memorial.

The first year was such a success that it has been repeated every year since. Two thirds of the money raised goes to nursing charities, Cancer Relief's Macmillan Nurses being the biggest beneficiary. The remaining third goes to The National Trust Garden Fund, the Gardeners' Royal Benevolent Society and the Royal Gardeners' Orphan Fund.

It is a most heartwarming and rewarding thought for those of us who share our gardens with our visitors, be it for one day, for a season, or all the year round, that we are making a contribution to people who well deserve our support.

This beautifully illustrated book, organized by Judy Johnson, well-observed by Susan Berry, photographed and sensitively put together by Steven Wooster, will, I hope, encourage many more to both open and visit gardens.

Beth Chatto

Authors' Preface

Once the idea had been mooted to devote a book to a cross-section of National Gardens Scheme gardens, we looked for ones which epitomized the appeal of so many in the Scheme. They could be small or large, but ideally they had to have the stamp of the owner's personality upon them, and preferably be gardened by the owners themselves.

Choosing the gardens from the thousands available was no simple task, and we are well aware that many others could and maybe should have been included. We hope, however, that our selection inspires readers to visit these and other gardens in the Scheme, and to bring back ideas for their own planting combinations.

This book could not have been produced without the help of Lt.-Col. D. G. Carpenter (retd.), the administrative staff at the National Gardens Scheme and all the County Organizers. We are immensely grateful to them and also to the owners who have generously allowed their gardens to be photographed, and who have given up their time to show us round.

The descriptions do not include opening times, directions or admission charges. Details of these and all other information about the gardens in the scheme can be found in the 'Yellow Book', *Gardens of England and Wales*, published by the National Gardens Scheme each year in February.

We hope that you enjoy reading about the gardens and, maybe, visiting them as much as we have enjoyed researching them.

Judy Johnson & Susan Berry

Opposite *The rose garden, Hazelby House*

Greencombe

Magnificent predominantly woodland garden, on a steep hillside, with a collection of rhododendrons, camellias, hydrangeas and ferns

SEEN IN THE late afternoon, when the sun is disappearing behind the hills backing Porlock Weir and the deep shadows and shafts of golden sunshine accentuate the myriad textures and forms of the foliage, Greencombe has a magical appeal. The current owner, Joan Loraine, is passionately involved in the garden and has developed and planted it over the years with consummate skill and great sensitivity.

It is not an easy garden, from either the plants' or the gardener's point of view. Stretched tight along a three-and-a-half-acre strip of land on the hillside overlooking Porlock Bay, it gets relatively little sun; the site is steep enough to make your legs ache, and there is virtually no natural soil, only many centuries worth of leaf-mould, created by the ancient woodland from which the garden has been sculpted.

The intention of the design was to make the garden an adventure and an experience, from the comparative formality around the house with 'its homely brick-path vegetable garden and rose-rich terraces,' in Joan Loraine's words, 'to the sheltered intimacy of the First Wood and the grey aisles of sweet chestnuts in the Far Wood beyond.'

The woodland is a splendid mixture of scales: the immense ancient sweet chestnuts and hollies rise high above you, creating a canopy for the many small woodland flowers, grasses and sedges that Joan Loraine has introduced, along with some notable small trees and shrubs and a much-loved collection of ferns.

Needless to say, rhododendrons flourish in the acid soil and damp woodland conditions. Greencombe has a rich and varied collection of several hundred of them, well worth travelling some distance to see in spring; but with so many rhododendrons, there is nearly always one in flower at any time of the year. Indeed, even in January, the garden is full of colour. As Joan Loraine writes in her lyrical introduction to the garden, 'the myriad gold petals of

The sloping lawn, above, looking across from the entrance to the woodland garden, towards the house, planted chiefly for contrasts of foliage and form.

The shady canopy, right, of the hollies, oaks and sweet chestnuts in the woodland area, together with the acid soil, provides an ideal home for many different azaleas.

•SOUTH WEST•

witch hazel (*Hamamelis mollis*) glisten against the purple-brown of leafless oak, and winter sweet (*Chimonanthus praecox*) hangs pale beside a 20-ft columnar cypress. *Rhododendron dauricum* . . . is a song of bright purple, *Camellia sasanqua* with its wild-rose flower, crimson and white varieties intertwined, is brilliant along the vegetable garden wall . . . and best of all, *Rhododendron gigant-eum* . . . with its wide trusses of bright rose magenta bells astride the foot-long, deeply veined leaves.'

For those who are interested in ferns, and Joan Loraine is one of them, they apparently grow like weeds at Greencombe. The conditions are ideal. A new path has been made in the wood which is lined with her polystichum collection, amongst which are planted cyclamen, erythroniums, trilliums and hellebores.

The wood is criss-crossed by small paths, allowing you the opportunity to examine the small woodland plants at your leisure. Miss Loraine is thrilled with one of her most recent acquisitions, *Viburnum alnifolium* (syn. *V. lantanoides*), which is not very easy to get hold of, but which has taken to the woodland setting with ease. One of the few acid-loving viburnums, it puts on a marvellous show of golden foliage in autumn. Another of her favourites is a *Vaccinium retusum* (described by Hillier as dwarf and shy-flowering) which scrambles happily to about 3 m (10 ft) up a neighbouring camellia, flowering prodigiously each year with graceful pink bells.

No gardener when she took Greencombe over, Joan Loraine says that the garden has taught her almost all she knows, along with the help and advice of a near neighbour, the RHS Victoria Medal holder Norman Hadden, who gardened at Underway in West Porlock. In the early days she would keep a notebook, filling it with questions and – when she had reached the bottom of a page – visiting Norman Hadden to get the answers.

As a memorial, she has a wonderful specimen of *Cornus* 'Porlock', now growing on the top boundary. A cross between *C. capitata* and *C. kousa*, created by the bumble-bees at Underway, it is a mass of edible cherry-like fruit every autumn. Among the other plants that do well in the terraces around the house are two different forms of myrtle, *M. luma* (syn. *Luma apiculata*), with its peeling red bark, and a more unusual one, *M. ugni* (now *Ugni molinae*), which has delicious small red fruit, tasting of wild strawberries.

Hydrangeas are another feature of the terraces, and no plant gives a longer season, as Miss Loraine points out. There are many very good blue hydrangeas that thrive on the acid soil at Greencombe, some of them turning shades of deep sea-green as the summer dies.

The neat dome of Acer palmatum *'Dissectum Atro-purpureum'*, *right, framed between the fastigiate Lawson's cypress on the left and the stout trunk of* Fothergilla major, *with* Erica arborea alpina *behind to its left.*

The apple tree bed, *left, on the lower lawn with primroses, dicentra, hellebores and the leaves of* Zantedeschia aethiopica *'Crowborough'.*

Fuchsia *'Tennessee Waltz'*, *above, and* Saxifraga fortunei, *backed by* Rhododendron calostrotum, *with a polystichum that has seeded itself — one of many that flourish in the garden.*

The Manor House

An English country garden with deep herbaceous borders and a fine small walled kitchen garden

THE MORE gardens you visit, the more you realize how much a successful marriage between the architecture of the house and the design of the garden contributes to the overall atmosphere.

The Manor House at Chaldon Herring is no exception. Lying in a fold of the Purbeck Hills, in former smuggling country close to Lulworth Cove, the house itself dates back to the reign of King John. The Fishburns, who bought the Manor House some fifteen years ago, inherited a beautiful house and a garden with a few promising structural features but little else. The singular unity of the garden and buildings is largely a result of Alice Fishburn's excellent eye for form, and her ability to keep her planting schemes restrained in both colour and style.

Pleached lime trees, underplanted with spring bulbs, flank the drive up to the house, and a gate through a small gravelled courtyard leads to the potager on one side of the house. This has been planted in cottage-garden style, mixing the flowers with the vegetables, but the espaliered apple trees bordering one side and the new beech hedge planted to provide shelter from

the roaring south-westerlies give just the right touch of architectural discipline. An informal border of flowers and herbs on one side of the kitchen garden has as its central feature a deep maroon moss rose (of unknown origin), which is trained into a dome shape by having its shoots tied down on to hazel wands.

Walking from the courtyard to the house, past the old harness room – now covered by a splendid *Clematis fargesii* (syn. *C. potaninii*) with its clusters of small white flowers in late summer – you get your first glimpse of Alice Fishburn's magnificent deep border, which is at its best in mid- to late July. It rises at the back to a good 2.5 m (8–9 ft), the height provided at intervals by roses, clematis and vines grown over frames and pillars, creating an almost swagged effect to the rear of the border. One of the most attractive combinations is *Rosa* 'François Juranville' with *Vitis vinifera* 'Purpurea'. The colour scheme is a soft tapestry of pinks, mauves, purples and blues, with delphiniums, phlox, astrantias, tradescantia, veronicas, geraniums, galega and the big *Campanula lactiflora* 'Loddon Anna', with dusky pink flowers.

A dark-red-flowered clematis, above, in full bloom, frames a seat. Mrs Fishburn first saw the clematis at Hidcote, and wishes that she knew its name.

The courtyard, right, with Rosa 'New Dawn' mingling with clematis and R. 'Madame Alfred Carrière' on the walls. In front of the wisteria-clad arch, alchemilla seeds itself.

Adding to the effect of height at the back of the border is a terrace, with a grassed path behind, surmounted by a thick clipped lonicera hedge. The path makes working in the border much easier, says Mrs Fishburn, but is not without its perils. While mowing it, both she and the mower once disappeared over the 60 cm (2 ft) drop into the plants below.

Running at right angles to the herbaceous border is a shrub border backed by a high brick wall. In it Mrs Fishburn is planting a number of attractive trees, with the idea that when she eventually grows too old to keep up the incessant hard work that the garden presently demands, she can turn it into a landscaped garden, French château style. A bricked-up arch in the high wall was

In a corner, *above, where the two borders meet, a clipped lonicera arch backs an unknown pink rose on a frame, christened* the 'Major's Rose' after the previous owner of the Manor House. In the foreground is the rose 'Gruss an Aachen'.

knocked through to reveal a wonderful view of the rolling landscape beyond, through a delicate filigree of wrought ironwork. Leading from the house towards the arch, in a stately march across the lawn, is a triple row of twelve large clipped yews. When the Fishburns took the garden over they were planted into borders, but the area has since been grassed over.

Among the other major changes they made was to divert the course of the drive from the front of the house to one side of it, and to terrace the area in front of the house. At the back they knocked out a room to create a courtyard, over which they have grown a magnificent vine, which not only provides much-needed shade in summer (it faces due south), but also crops abundantly in autumn. Around the house, they planted 'Madame Alfred Carrière' roses, seven of them, which now create great swathes of foliage and scented, creamy white flowers from summer to early autumn. They intermingle in June and July with the blooms of *Clematis* 'Perle d'Azur' and in September with *Clematis rehderiana* – a solid mass of cowslip-like buff flowers on a large pergola over the east side of the house – underplanted with *Hydrangea paniculata* 'Tardiva', the white flowers of which gleam out like candles in the deep shade.

At the front of the house, facing north, are several plants of *Rosa glauca* (better known as *R. rubrifolia*), their blue-green foliage mingling well with that of a *Vitis vinifera* 'Purpurea' (which manages to form good clumps of grapes even on a really cold wall), and an *Akebia quinata*, another good climber for a north-facing wall, with vanilla-scented purplish flowers. The beds are planted with two large shrubs of the soft grey-leaved *Senecio* (now *Brachyglottis*) *greyi*, different hostas, astrantias, pulmonarias and *Viola bertolonii*. Mrs Fishburn calls the latter her 'Desert Island' choice, as she would loathe to be without it. She particularly enjoys the way it will climb through other plants like geraniums.

The Hybrid Musk rose 'Felicia', left, provides the focal point in an informal border in the kitchen garden. On its left is a deep maroon rose of unknown origin, and in front are several forms of geranium, including G. psilostemon, G. phaeum *and* G. 'Johnson's Blue', *with alchemilla and* Viola cornuta.

The view over the lawn, above, past the Irish yews, from the rockery steps, over which sprawl campanula and ferns.

Milton Lodge

A terraced garden with splendid views of the surrounding countryside, and a collection of interesting trees, shrubs and perennials

O N THE southern slopes of the Mendip Hills with panoramic views of Wells Cathedral and the Vale of Avalon, the gardens at Milton Lodge have been created on several levels. The house itself, an attractive eighteenth-century stone building, has been added to over the years and belonged originally to the current owner's grandfather, before it became a school in the War years, when the garden was, like so many others, badly neglected.

Mr and Mrs Tudway Quilter came to live here in 1958 and it took them nearly eight years to get the garden back into shape. Apart from its fine formal terraces, it has a splendid collection of trees (the Tudway Quilters also have an arboretum just down the road) and magnificent yew hedges planted around 1900, over which you can see parkland stretching away to the Cathedral.

In front of the house, facing south, is a handsome stone terrace and a small formal lawn. The four cannon ranged along the terrace wall were signal cannon from French battleships in the

Napoleonic war, and were once sited in the garden of the family house in the Liberty in Wells, which now forms part of the Cathedral School. Now strategically aimed towards the Cathedral, they act, in Mr Tudway Quilter's words, 'as a defence against any untoward sorties by the Dean and Chapter'. At the end of the terrace stands a large *Clerodendrum trichotomum*. The parent of a number of others in the garden, it has fragrant white flowers in September, followed by china-blue berries. Near by a large mahonia, like the clerodendrum, is over a quarter of a century old, and farther along the terrace the red flowers of *Salvia × grahamii* rise above a collection of grey-leaved perennial plants.

A grass path leads on from the terrace along this upper level, to a small tree collection, which the Tudway Quilters planted soon after their arrival. Among the oldest trees, dating from 1967, are a weeping white lime (*Tilia* 'Petiolaris'), a Turkey oak (*Quercus cerris*), a fern-leaved beech (*Fagus sylvatica* 'Heterophylla', syn.

The panoramic view, *above, of Wells Cathedral and the Vale of Avalon, framed by a pair of* Chamaecyparis lawsoniana, *seen from the upper terrace in front of the house.*

Repeating clumps, *right, of the brilliant purple-flowered* Geranium × magnificum *punctuate the herbaceous border at the foot of the wall on the lower terrace.*

Two small cherubs, *above,
backed by the pink-flowered
valerian (*Centranthus ruber*),
which self-seeds on the
chalky soil, and* Potentilla
'Vilmoriniana'.

'Asplenifolia'), white poplars (*Populus alba*) and a fine group of white willows (*Salix alba*). Autumn colour is well represented by parrotia, several maples, including *Acer griseum* and *A. saccharinum*, and a *Crataegus* 'Prunifolia'.

East of the arboretum, and on the same level, is the big lower lawn with a swimming pool and pavilion at one end and a huge two-hundred-year-old oak tree at the other. A long mixed border runs the length of the retaining wall, crowned by the yew hedge and clothed with clematis, ceanothus, rhamnus and the rich yellow rose 'Royal Gold'. The border planting is given structure by massive clumps of potentilla and *Fuchsia magellanica* 'Alba', and at each end the white flowers of *Philadelphus coronarius* 'Variegatus' fill the air with their heady scent for three weeks in summer.

A yew hedge 72 m (80 yd) long borders the lawn on the other side, beyond which a fenced grass walk abuts the parkland, and

leads to the wilder part of the garden immediately below the house terrace. In spring, this area is a brilliant splash of colour with daffodils, bluebells, cowslips, primroses and moon daisies.

From both ends of the lower lawn, steps lead up to a long, rather narrow terrace with a deep border of shrub roses against the terrace wall, underplanted with hardy geraniums, lamium, epilobium, *Anthemis cupaniana* and the deep blue dwarf plumbago (*Ceratostigma plumbaginoides*). These not only provide ground cover for the roses but also soften the stone edging to the border.

From this terrace more steps lead up to the gently sloping central lawn, surrounded by mixed borders of shrubs and herbaceous plants. At the lower end, along the terrace wall, 'Frensham' roses stand to attention like a line of scarlet-coated sentries. On the red brick wall at the back are trained the white-flowered *Escallonia* 'Iveyi', *Abutilon vitifolium*, *Abelia* × *grandiflora* and a vast variegated euonymus planted before the War, as well as a fine specimen of the South American *Feijoa* (now *Acca*) *sellowiana*. In these borders are some particularly good plant associations including *Crocosmia* 'Lucifer' with purple berberis and the dark crimson *Knautia macedonica* against the grey leaves of *Olearia macrodonta*. In one corner, drifts of *Romneya coulteri* root themselves freely among the shrubs, their golden-centred white poppy flowers providing a star turn in the summer months.

A gateway leads into the courtyard where teas and plants from the garden are sold on open days. A giant golden yew towers over the steps leading to the upper terrace, and overhangs a *Cotoneaster franchetii*, laden with pollen-rich flowers in summer and masses of scarlet berries in autumn and winter.

The perfect *icing-sugar-pink papery flowers of everyone's favourite rose, 'Fantin-Latour', far left.*

The daisy *Anthemis cupaniana, left, interplanted with alliums along the lower terrace.*

Chyverton

Landscaped garden with magnificent woodland planting, including many rare and exotic trees and shrubs

IF YOU LIKE camellias, magnolias and rhododendrons, as well as gardens that imitate nature fairly closely, then Chyverton is a must. Set in about twenty acres of attractively landscaped park and woodland, a few miles inland from the north Cornish coast, the gardens were laid out in the eighteenth century. The large ornamental lake, with its handsome stone bridge, and the predominantly shrub and tree planting recall Stourhead, without its formality.

Mr and Mrs Nigel Holman inherited the garden from Mr Holman's father in 1963 and since then have added at least a hundred new genera to what was already an impressive collection. For some reason plants from Chile seem to do particularly well at Chyverton. The long myrtle hedge (*Myrtus luma* – now *Luma apiculata*) with its glorious, rusty red shredding bark is justly famous as the only one of its kind in Britain. Now about 6 m (20 ft) high, the only pruning it gets is the removal of the small branches to expose the bark on the main ones. Illuminated by the setting sun, it is a sight worth travelling some distance to see, and enough apparently to inspire Roy Lancaster, on one of his visits to Chyverton, to dance a jig through the middle of it.

Among the other immigrants from Chile are the evergreen *Azara lanceolata*, with its clusters of yellow flowers in spring, and *Laurelia serrata*, with leaves that are delightfully aromatic when crushed, with a scent of oranges and aniseed. A *Nothofagus dombeyi*, planted in 1980, has now grown into a splendid tree with beautiful bark and an attractive habit.

The gardens have a subtle, insidious charm, which the Holmans put down to the contrast of all the greens, which are very soft, under the particular intensity of the Cornish light. They are laid out as a series of informal 'rooms' joined by mown paths. The bluebells contribute to the natural atmosphere of the garden, and are not cut down until after they have seeded themselves.

A lichen-covered bridge, above, in the woodland area near the drive is strongly reminiscent of Monet's one at Giverny. Behind are the feathery forms of Erica erigena *and the creamy yellow* Corylopsis pauciflora.

Mown grass paths, right, lead into a number of small clearings, each with a different planting character. In this area Acer palmatum atropurpureum *is partnered by* Rhododendron *'Winsome'.*

Apart from the collection of camellias, magnolias and rhododendrons for which Chyverton is justly famous, there are many other rare trees and shrubs which survive in Cornwall's almost subtropical climate. The tender *Magnolia dealbata* from Mexico, with enormous leaves like a coconut palm, is so far coping well in a sheltered part of the garden. The leaves are reputed to make a marvellous remedy for sprains, when applied as a poultice, but the Holmans have yet to put this to the test.

Among the other exotics is a splendid example of *Dicksonia antarctica*, the Australian tree fern, with its stout trunk and palm-like fronds, and *Dacrydium* (now *Lagarostrobos*) *franklinii*, the Huon pine from Tasmania, with its attractively drooping branches. Nyssas also do well in the garden, including *N. sylvatica* and *N. sinensis*. Several are beginning to come from root suckers, one of which Mr Holman successfully transplanted, amazing a visitor from France, who said it could not be done.

The Holmans have planted about thirty different species of maple, including the snakebark maple (*Acer davidii*), *A. forrestii*, *A. cissifolium* and *A. campbellii*, in part to provide good autumn colour although they also make attractive spring growth.

CULTIVATION
Myrtle

UNDER the collective heading of myrtles come a number of attractive half-hardy evergreen shrubs or trees. *M.ugni (Ugni molinae)*, a shrubby form to about 1.8m (6ft), makes good dense hedging with the bonus of delicious fruit. *M. luma* (below left), which grows to about 9m (30ft) if left unpruned, has attractively peeling bark. They grow best in full sun.

The peeling bark of the myrtle hedge (Myrtus luma, *syn.* Luma apiculata), *left, catches the setting sun.*

Bluebells *are encouraged to self-seed at Chyverton, and the grass paths are not mown until after they have died down. Here, far left, they surround a venerable* Magnolia sprengeri.

Chilcombe House

*Hillside garden with compartmentalized design,
exuberant and well-planned planting and
spectacular views*

T HE SETTING at Chilcombe has the sense of peace that you tend to find only in old monasteries. The original settlement dates back to Domesday, and the foundations of the former manor house are still clearly visible just beyond the existing garden walls. John and Caryl Hubbard have been at Chilcombe House since 1969. When they took it over, there was no garden to speak of: simply the walls, and a lawn sloping down to one side of the house. To begin with they improved the part near the house, a little at a time, and then established the double border in the middle of the garden. The next step was to divide it into quarters with a cross path down the other axis, at right angles, and to put in the mixed marbled hedge, with two sorts of beech, two sorts of yew and so on. In those days the flower elements were chiefly confined to the double border and the parts near the house. Gradually the emphasis has changed, the vegetables have given way to more flowers, and the original divisions have been subdivided again.

The garden has been laid out with a clear sense of geometry, providing a counterpoint to the relaxed and free nature of the planting. According to Mr Hubbard, maintaining the right balance between formality and informality is the key to successful garden design. You need to be reminded of the basic geometry – something absent, he feels, in gardens with curving beds, for which he has a particular dislike.

Although there were several trees on the site, including the large ornamental cherry by the gate, the Hubbards have planted many more. A deep herbaceous border with large clumps of perennials with attractive foliage faces the house on one side of the wall that separates off the lawned area. A gateway overhung by the arching branches of *Buddleja alternifolia* takes you into the double border, which slopes gently down, giving wonderful views of the hills and valleys beyond. It is backed by old-fashioned roses such as 'Reine des Violettes', and enclosed with espaliered apples and pears on rustic frames, through which twist a variety of clematis.

In the walled garden, above, the deep purple flowers of Clematis 'Ville de Lyon' *mingle with those of an unknown rose.*

In the same area, right, 'Tour de Malakoff' and 'Goldfinch' roses scramble over a pergola, with lavender, actaea, violas and giant bleeding heart below.

CULTIVATION
Arches and tunnels

LIVING walkways, arches and tunnels can be created by growing plants over appropriate supports, which can vary to suit the garden, from simple rustic poles to elaborate wrought ironwork. Climbers are obvious candidates but even trees can be trained to shape by being pruned and tied in. Overhead features in kitchen gardens are both productive and ornamental, bearing crops of apples, pears and grapes or supporting decorative vegetables like marrows and runner beans. But purely ornamental planting of, say, wisteria or laburnum (each with long racemes of flowers) or of roses and clematis entwined together, creates a romantic atmosphere. Until the more slow-growing plants cover the framework, nasturtiums or sweet peas can be grown up it.

To one side of the double border is a formal section with vivid blue 'Crater Lake' veronicas, and white iris, and a white standard wisteria. Beyond it the garden rises to a higher level, with a splendid thyme bank that the Hubbards have gradually created over the years. In the space where a venerable apple tree once created a natural visual screen between the levels, the Hubbards have planted *Crambe cordifolia* with its 1.8 m (6 ft)-tall clouds of white flowers and large crinkled leaves while they wait for the replacement apple tree to grow. Roses grow on the high walls that surround this end of the garden, and at their feet are large clumps of *Phygelius aequalis* in pinkish red and pale yellow.

The potager in the section below is now laid out in cottage-garden style with a mixture of flowers and vegetables, the brick paths neatly edged with old stone roof tiles. Beyond the potager is a small buddleja grove which the Hubbards have now turned into a woodland walk, and beyond it is the orchard, where the old fruit trees serve primarily as supports for vigorous climbing roses, such as 'Rambling Rector', 'Seagull' and 'Bobbie James'. In the section beyond the orchard the Hubbards grow the greatest variety of herbaceous plants, among them thirty or more different salvias, including their own *Salvia patens* 'Chilcombe' with attractive mauve flowers.

Closer to the house there is a small courtyard garden where plants have been allowed to self-seed in the cracks in the paving — a form of 'orchestrated chaos', according to John Hubbard — while beyond it is a recently created wild garden, hedged with sea buckthorn, with a central mown path. The Hubbards are happy with the balance of grasses and wild flowers in the planting.

The double border, *left, with roses 'Little White Pet', 'Yesterday', 'Ispahan', and 'Souvenir du Doctor Jamain' and salvias and cardoons.*

The vista *down to the vegetable garden, right. The grass path is lined with irises,* Nepeta nervosa *and* Malva moschata *'Alba'.*

Putsborough Manor

*Thatched manor house with a large walled garden,
with a variety of features, including double
borders, herb garden and stream planting*

EVEN VISITED on a wet day, and seen from under the shelter of a large umbrella, Putsborough Manor still exerts a powerful charm. The hamlet of Putsborough, less than a mile inland from the north Devon coast, is a picture-book Devon village, complete with pond, ducks and a visiting heron. The Manor itself, one of several closely grouped thatched houses, apparently dates back to a Saxon settlement, although it has been rebuilt since then. Nevertheless, the roof in the barn is pre-Elizabethan, the underpart of the thatching untouched since it was first constructed, with the straw tied on to the rough-hewn roof timbers.

The garden is divided into two parts, at the front and back of the house. At the front, set into the lawn, is a magnificent and ancient mulberry tree (in all probability around three hundred years old) which was once struck by lightning. It has since created a fascinating knot of branches which have rerooted where they touched the ground; it now not only has a beautiful spreading

shape but also still continues to produce far more mulberries each year than can easily be disposed of.

Behind the mulberry tree (where the original drive had been) is a shady area alongside the boundary wall, bordered by a rushing stream and overhung by lime trees and a large beech. On the banks, in spring, are massed bulbs – crocuses, irises and fritillaries – and lots of candelabra primulas. There are also hydrangeas, large clumps of grasses, and other shade-loving plants, including the Californian hybrid iris in two shades of mauve, which come out very early and continue until long into the year.

Near the mulberry tree is a paulownia, planted about nine years ago, which has delighted everyone in the last two springs with a mass of lovely blue foxglove-like flowers. The herbaceous borders that fringe the sweep of lawn (much used for games of croquet in the summer) are backed by the stone walls that enclose this part of the garden in a rough semi-circle. Against the backdrop of the house walls, themselves clad in an attractive clipped

Silvery pink heads of allium, above, blend perfectly with those of self-seeding foxgloves in an informal border.

The handsome cream-edged leaves of Hosta crispula, right, marry successfully with those of Zantedeschia aethiopica 'Crowborough' in the moist, shady stream borders.

The apple arbour, *above,*
of mixed eating and crab
apples, underplanted with
aquilegias and later-flowering
osteospermums.

myrtle (*Myrtus communis*), is a striking formal border of grey-leaved plants, such as lamb's ears (*Stachys lanata* – now *S. byzantina*) interplanted with the brilliant scarlet Floribunda rose 'Sarabande' that blooms from June till November.

The design and planting of the garden have evolved over the years since Mr and Mrs Bigge took it over. The garden rises quite sharply on the east side, and for some time they were not sure how to tackle the marriage of the two levels. Then a friend brought the late Peter Coats to visit, who put into words what they had already had in mind to do: create a sloping bed for alpine and rock plants between the two areas of grass. The sweep of the beds now satisfactorily echoes the contours of the surrounding walls, and provides space for spring and summer colour from plants like the

hardy perennial *Pulsatilla vulgaris*, some of them self-sown, various varieties of cistus, campanula and viola, and some of the smaller dianthus, interspersed with larger plantings of verbena and *Diascia barberiae* with its rose-pink flowers.

In the top border, near the gardener's cottage, is a wide bed, with climbing roses, honeysuckle and clematis on the wall behind, and peonies, astrantia, asters and yet more roses in front. On the actual wall of the cottage is a venerable *Magnolia grandiflora*, with its spectacular large bowl-shaped scented white flowers from midsummer until autumn, and its equally attractive large glossy green leaves. Mr and Mrs Bigge are very fond of magnolias, but this one is among the few that will grow on the limy soil at Putsborough.

On the back wall of the house is the exotic *Campsis grandiflora*, with its huge trumpet-shaped orange and red flowers in late summer; while in the central courtyard, within the rectangle formed by the house, cottage and barn, are massed hydrangeas and roses.

To the rear, in what was formerly the kitchen garden, there is now a semi-formal flower garden and a vegetable garden. Handsome double borders lead up, on either side of a grass walk, to an arbour of apple and crab apple trees that bisects the rear part of the garden. The border itself has a number of Shrub and Floribunda roses, and is backed on each side by a hedge of the wonderfully scented white rose 'Penelope', grown on frames.

To one side of the arbour is an attractive herb garden with a fruit cage beyond, and behind these is an orchard, underplanted with spring bulbs. On the other side is a prolific vegetable garden, divided from the rest of the garden by hedges of escallonia.

The area, *left, in front of the gardener's cottage with its informal mixture of herbaceous perennials. Geraniums, cistus and daisies of different types combine with pink tulips and agapanthus, backed by the shrub rose 'Fantin-Latour'.*

CULTIVATION
Silver and grey foliage

Among the best silver-leaved plants for full sun are *Achillea* 'Moonshine', *Artemisia absinthium* 'Lambrook Silver' (pale yellow flowers), *Ballota pseudodictamnus, Baptisia australis* (blue flowers), *Stachys byzantina* and *Helichrysum petiolare* (white flowers). Larger perennials include *Melianthus major, Onopordum acanthium* and *Euphorbia characias wulfenii.*

An elegant silver and red planting scheme, right, makes a perfect foil for the front of the house. The Floribunda rose 'Sarabande' is underplanted with a range of silver-leaved plants including Stachys byzantina, artemisias, arabis and Convolvulus cneorum, while Clematis 'Comtesse de Bouchaud' adorns the thatched porch.

Pear Tree House

Wide-spreading garden with many fine trees and shrubs, and excellent contrasts of foliage form and texture

ALL GARDENERS, according to John and Pam Southwell, are motivated by two conflicting aims: to collect as many interesting plants as possible and to create an aesthetically pleasing garden. The Southwells have managed to perform a successful balancing act at Pear Tree House. Although the ancient pear tree that gave the cottage its name has since been lost, they have more than compensated for its disappearance with a much-prized collection of trees, particularly hollies, acers, birches and willows, as well as a wide range of shrubs, roses, clematis and herbaceous perennials.

The gardens surround the house, on a long thin parcel of land bordering a lane, and now cover around three and a half acres, much of it reclaimed from meadow land, the newer parts simply added as time and circumstance allowed.

The Southwells tackled the area around the house first, creating a cottage garden which originally owed much to Margery Fish's influence, her garden at East Lambrook Manor being within easy visiting distance. A stone path bisects the cottage garden, and on either side are thickly planted perennials, including the burning bush (*Dictamnus albus purpureus*), with its pink flower spikes that release volatile oils in the evening, verbascums, achillea, delphiniums and eremurus. They are backed by some attractive variegated shrubs, including *Cornus mas* 'Variegata' with its silvery-edged foliage and a variegated ligustrum, with its yellow-bordered evergreen leaves.

In the late summer this part of the garden enjoys a second display with *Aster amellus*, phlox, heleniums and sidalcea all in flower. The dry stone wall bordering the cottage garden has been rebuilt and is used as support for many different clematis and roses. Although these beds were originally designed to house small treasures, they are not, as John Southwell points out, so little any more. Among the larger herbaceous perennials is *Veratrum nigrum* with its leaves like pleated Fortuny silk, *Actaea alba*, an unusual perennial with fluffy white flowers, and the double Canadian bloodroot (*Sanguinaria canadensis* 'Plena'), tovara, *Saxifraga fortunei* 'Wada' and numerous hostas.

*A **sheltered spot** to sit, above, shaded by an old apple tree, one of several that the Southwells inherited with the garden.*

*The **sculptural forms**, right, of grasses such as varieties of* Miscanthus sinensis *(from left, 'Zebrinus', 'Silberfeder' and 'Gracillimus').*

On the other side of the cottage garden wall is a bed primarily intended for foliage plants, particularly those with gold or purple leaves. It includes a golden berberis, the moonlight holly (*Ilex aquifolium* 'Flavescens'), a yellow thalictrum and *Ptelea trifoliata* 'Aurea' with sweetly scented flowers. Immediately behind the house is the first pond that the Southwells made, using a butyl liner. Thickly planted around its margins are a number of bog garden plants, like astilbes, *Primula florindae*, rodgersias, rheums (*R.* 'Bowles' Crimson' and *R. alexandrae*) and a yellow bamboo. Some of the more unusual acers are planted here too, including *A. cissifolium*, a small Japanese maple with bronzy leaves, and *A. henryi*, an elegant spreading Chinese maple with grey-striped bark.

Beyond the pond is a small hidden garden, tucked behind a tall purple beech hedge. Near by is a small plantation of species roses, including *Rosa californica* 'Plena' with its double, scented pink flowers and Wolley-Dod's rose, a semi-double with attractive red hips. A former apple orchard close by now houses the overspill from John Southwell's particular obsession – an ever-increasing collection of hollies. Also in this part of the garden is a form of the Chinese tulip tree (*Liriodendron chinense*) with large lobed leaves, suffused purple in spring, and a variegated one, *L. tulipifera* 'Aureomarginatum', plus a collection of conifers.

Farther down the garden, near another ornamental pool, the Southwells have planted giant grasses, and created an acer glade with some spectacular forms, including *Acer* 'Worleei', with its almost luminous yellow leaves, *A. cappadocicum* 'Aureum' and *A. c.* 'Rubrum', as well as *A. rubrum* 'Schlesingeri' with its brilliant red autumn foliage and *A. platanoides* 'Fascens Black'.

Beyond them is John Southwell's special collection of hollies. The wide range comes as a surprise to many gardeners, whose contact with them in garden centres is probably limited to the more common forms like *Ilex* 'Silver Queen' and 'Golden King'.

CULTIVATION
Hollies for the small garden

Nearly all hollies are slow-growing and can be clipped, so they are good subjects where there is not much space to spare. *Ilex altaclerensis* 'Lawsoniana' is one of the most attractively leaved hollies, readily available from nurseries, and with a tendency to form a bush; *I. aquifolium* 'Wateriana', also variegated, is compact and slow-growing. *I.a.* 'Hastata' and *I. pernyi* tend to be narrow in habit and have curiously shaped small leaves. *I. cornuta* 'Lydia Morris' forms a rounded bush.

All the *Ilex crenata* group are small (some miniature) and suitable for rock gardens. *I.c.* 'Fukarin' (syn. 'Shiro-fukurin') with apple-green/grey leaves and *I.c.* 'Convexa" with glossy convex leaves are both worth looking out for.

The statue *of Hebe, left, framed by the nut hedge (*Corylus maxima *'Purpurea').*

Ken-Caro

Fine flowering shrubs are the hallmark of this well-planned and planted Cornish garden

VISITORS to Ken-Caro often make the mistake, when they see all the rhododendrons and camellias in flower, of thinking that it is predominantly a spring garden. Although it is spectacular in the early part of the year, Mr and Mrs Willcock have actually planned it for year-round colour. They have an abiding love of beautiful plants and have filled the garden with some particularly attractive flowering shrubs, set off to perfection against the rolling views of Dartmoor in the distance.

They do indeed have a number of rhododendrons, in species and dwarf forms in particular, and some fine camellias as well as a range of pieris, since the soil is very acid, like many of the Cornish gardens. *Pieris formosa forrestii*, especially, is exquisite in spring, with its blush-coloured new leaf growth and panicles of creamy flowers. The soil is also naturally fairly light at Ken-Caro, and needs a lot of manure worked into it to help retain the moisture that the shrubs need, particularly when they are young.

The Willcocks manage to grow a good collection of hostas, which are normally said to prefer damp shade. They do have to pick the site for the variegated ones, to prevent the sun from scorching the leaves. In one bed the hostas have been mixed with various dicentras, of which *D. eximia alba*, which goes on and on producing its white flowers, and *D. e.* 'Boothmans' with its steely blue foliage and dusky pink flowers are two of the best.

Another bed is devoted to spiky-leaved plants, with several different forms of iris, including *Iris kaempferi* (now *I. ensata*), tradescantia, and a number of crocosmias, including a particularly handsome one from Ireland, 'George Davidson'.

As the Willcocks are professional flower arrangers, they are particularly fond of their very free-flowering *Abutilon* × *suntense*, which produces literally hundreds of its papery blue flowers every spring. (They offered a useful flower arranging tip: if you want to preserve the sprays, scrape a bit of bark off the bottom, wrap the blossom loosely in a large tea towel, and boil the end of the stem

Contrasts of form and foliage, above. The drooping Chamaecyparis obtusa *'Nana Gracilis' is set off by the dark green* C. pisifera *'Filifera Aurea' and the tall pillar of the* C. lawsoniana *'Kilmacurragh' beyond.*

Rhododendrons, right, flourish in the damp, acid conditions in Cornwall. Just coming into bloom on the left is R. *'Joseph Whitworth', with 'Marchioness of Lansdowne' and 'Pink Cherub' beyond.*

Spiky-leaved plants, left, like the Yucca gloriosa *'Variegata' in the centre of the picture, are much liked by the Willcocks, who also have a bed devoted to them. They enjoy the contrast of form with the rhododendrons, here 'Cynthia' on the left and 'Bagshot Ruby' on the right.*

The brilliant spring growth, left, of Pieris formosa forrestii *on the left of the picture and the cream-edged leaves of* Hosta crispula *make a handsome frame for the little statue in a corner of the garden.*

for a couple of minutes. The spray will then last for ten days. This works with other woody-stemmed plants too, like beech.) They also have an *Abutilon vitifolium album*.

Among their other favourite flowering plants are the spectacular tree peony 'Mrs William Kellway', which produces its soup-plate-size white flowers in spring, but the season is very short. They need shelter, and plenty of bonemeal, and ideally a heavy soil, which the Willcocks provide with old farmyard manure.

Among the more unusual plants in the garden is a *Lomatia ferruginea*, now ten years old, which is now about 4.5 m (15 ft) high. It makes a handsome evergreen, with reddish woody stems and scarlet flowers in high summer, almost hidden by the foliage. They are not apparently as tender as people have been led to believe, according to Mr Willcock, and would make a good subject for a small London garden.

Among the many attractive camellias is 'Anticipation' with its deep rose flowers, 'Joan Trehane' with a loose habit and large peony-like orchid-pink blooms, and 'Brigadoon', covered with very large semi-double pink flowers.

The structural planting is provided by a range of interesting conifers (including the slim and elegant *Chamaecyparis lawsoniana* 'Kilmacurragh' and the golden-leaved 'Buckland Gold') plus some attractive mature trees, including several maples – *Acer pseudoplatanus* 'Leopoldii', *A. platanoides* 'Drummondii', *A. p.* 'Crimson King' and *A. cappadocicum* (with its wonderful golden autumn colour) – as well as a crinodendrum and a Chilean fire bush (*Embothrium coccineum*). A number of plants with variegated foliage give year-round interest in the garden, including *Aralia elata* 'Variegata', *Aucuba* 'Golden Spangles', *Pittosporum* 'Irene Paterson' and a collection of phormiums.

Sticky Wicket

*A recently planted garden with a
Jekyllesque flower garden, arranged
in concentric rings, as its centrepiece*

CREATED within the last four years from a corner of a field, the garden at Sticky Wicket already has a surprisingly mature air about it. The Lewises work as a team, but the responsibility for the design and planting is Mrs Lewis's preserve. The garden now occupies about a third of the three-acre site, although at the outset only the area immediately surrounding the house was planted. Later came the large flower garden which encircles a sundial set in a camomile lawn and, on a long finger of land beside the paddock, the nursery and vegetable garden.

For visitors, the flower garden is the chief attraction, its beds arranged quite formally in concentric circles and divided by gravel paths. A Jekyllesque sense of colour pervades this part of the garden, where Mrs Lewis has taken great pains to search out specific species and cultivars to ensure that the flower colours create subtle, almost imperceptible shifts of tone. So one bed will be devoted to deep rose pinks, the next to paler pinks and creams, the next to creams and pale yellows, and so on. Red has been eschewed, wisely, because it draws the eye and is out of sympathy with the otherwise harmonious colour tones.

One of the more attractive aspects of the planting is that Mrs Lewis is also happy to let plants self-seed in the right situation, and among the plants that flourish here are mulleins and evening primroses, lupins and foxgloves.

There is a strong emphasis on silver-leaved plants and variegated foliage – *Lamium maculatum* 'Beacon Silver', silver-leaved thyme and variegated vinca, as well as santolina, teucrium and lavender – which provide a useful backdrop for the delicate flower colours.

Mrs Lewis has a weakness for scented plants – honeysuckle abounds in the garden in many forms, and the flower garden in particular has many scented and aromatic plants planted close to the paths so that you release the fragrance as you brush past.

Partly through her ecological interests, and partly because she likes to have something happening at every season, Mrs Lewis has included a great many plants with coloured stems, autumn and winter foliage colour, and with hips and berries. Unusually, although there is a reserved area for fruit, raspberry and loganberry canes, and blackberries, have been planted among the shrubs, to provide interest and to allow you to sample the fruit as you pass.

*The spectacular starry flower heads of the
common leek, above, are perfect with the
purplish heads of the globe artichoke.*

*The flower garden, right, with its sundial
set in a camomile lawn. In the foreground are
Welsh onions, sage and lavender.*

CULTIVATION
Decorative edible plants

Vegetables and fruit can be included very successfully in the flower border, and many of the commonly grown ones are surprisingly attractive in flower, including rhubarb and leeks. Many others are both edible and ornamental. Oak-leaved lettuces, chives and parsley make a neat edging for a flower border; gooseberries can be trained into shapely standards for a potager, and soft fruits such as raspberries, loganberries and redcurrants can be grown over rustic poles to make an attractive backdrop to a border. To crop well, all fruit and vegetables need plenty of humus and moisture, and a sunny site.

Fitz House

*A terraced garden, whose formal
framework contains an exuberant
mixture of roses and perennials*

A DELIGHTFUL blend of formal design and romantic planting, the gardens at Fitz House surround a much-admired group of sixteenth- and seventeenth-century stone buildings. The bones of the design were laid out in the 1920s, and the garden, under Major and Mrs Mordaunt-Hare's care for the last forty years, has filled out and flourished. The framework, like an Edwardian lady's stays, is now struggling to hold in the exuberance of the planting.

In the more formal areas around the house and outbuildings, spilling over the paths and softening their angles, are enthusiastically self-seeding mounds of *Alchemilla mollis* and the starry blue-flowered *Campanula poscharskyana*, a combination that works surprisingly well against the muted colour of the stone.

The small circular formal rose garden to the side of the house has been planted with 'Frensham' roses, underplanted with *Lavandula angustifolia* 'Munstead'. Unlike the modern roses, these early 'Frenshams' never suffer from mildew, and the strong bluish tones of the deep red flowers make an arresting contrast with the dark purple spikes of the lavender and the greyish stone surrounds.

Filling this area of the garden with the redolent scent of its leaves is *Rosa primula*, known as the incense rose for reasons that are immediately apparent. Its smallish flowers come out early but it is well worth growing for the scent of the leaves alone. If the scent of the roses and lavender were not enough, a couple of 'citron' day-lilies (*Hemerocallis citrina*), with their handsome soft yellow flowers, add their contribution to the heady pot-pourri.

An arch into the garden behind the house provides a support for the dark-leaved *Vitis vinifera* 'Purpurea', which turns deep purple late in the season, with a *Clematis* 'Perle d'Azur' climbing through it, one of the many in this garden that twist their way over every form of support.

A rectangular lawn with herbaceous borders and another small rose garden, tucked behind a very tall beech hedge, make up the more formal surrounds to the house. A bed of 'Peace' roses in

*The winged cherub, above, holding a fish,
stands on a plinth which once saw service
as an old cider press. He makes the centrepiece
of a small pool in the rose garden (shown
opposite in summer).*

*A sea of 'Frensham' roses and lavender
(*Lavandula *'Munstead'), right, makes a
striking contrast with the grey stone
statuary. At the cherub's feet are bowls
of* Helichrysum petiolare *and blue lobelia.*

CULTIVATION
Alchemilla mollis

ONE OF the most useful ground-covering plants, *Alchemilla mollis* will grow in any moist, well-drained soil in either full sun or partial shade. It forms generous clumps with attractive light green hand-shaped leaves and spires of yellowish-green flowers from mid- to late summer. It self-seeds freely, which is fine when needed as ground cover, but if you want to prevent it spreading, simply cut it back after flowering. Clumps of alchemilla can be divided and replanted any time between autumn and spring, or alternatively it can be grown from seed, sown in March and pricked out later as seedlings, and planted out in autumn. A smaller species, *A. alpina*, with green flowers and small neat leaves, is equally attractive.

muted colours forms the central point of the second rose garden, but Major and Mrs Mordaunt-Hare feel that Edwardian ones would be more in keeping. So far, though, the temptation to replace them has been resisted, because they are doing so well.

In the borders around the rose garden are large clumps of blue and pink penstemons that do well on the greensand on which Fitz House is based. It also gives plenty of choice as to what can be grown — even azaleas, which add spring colour — in a region which is otherwise chalk-based. Blue meconopsis flourish in a shady corner here, as do *sieboldiana* hostas, while on the sunnier side a scented 'Blanche Double de Coubert' rose, a half-standard 'The Fairy', an American honeysuckle and a weigela do well.

Around the lawn behind the house the borders have a predominantly silver, pink, blue and white theme, made up of, amongst

Alchemilla mollis, *far left, lines a path in front of the barn, at the foot of which are the yellow flowers of Jerusalem sage* (Phlomis fruticosa) *with 'citron' day-lilies. Clematis and roses cover the barn wall in summer, and the foliage of the vine trained over the arch on the far right turns a rich reddish purple later in the year.*

Two Ali Baba jars, *left, along with statuesque verbascums, stand sentinel at the top of the garden, looking down towards the house. Rosa 'Kew Rambler' covers the arch on the left; beneath it is the climbing rose 'Meg'.*

others, clumps of the magnificent silvery pink flowered, large-leaved *Salvia sclarea turkestanica* (the crushed leaves of which, according to gardening writer Robin Lane Fox, smell like a roomful of sweaty Samurai warriors!), many geraniums, including a pretty and vigorous white-flowered one by the steps, lychnis, pink and white valerian, more campanulas, old-fashioned roses and clematis, and a beautiful white phlox flanking a seat. Wild strawberries, campanula and small-flowered geraniums sprawl lazily underfoot across the steps and terraces, indeed almost everywhere you tread.

On the terraces above the lawn, studded with valerian and helianthemums, are arches and frames providing support for the free association of clematis, ornamental vines and roses, as well as late Dutch honeysuckle and sweet peas. A grass walk is lined with *Rosa* 'Lady Godiva' on a looped frame, under which a row of verbascums have seeded themselves in almost military formation, making an unusual but effective combination. Ahead, the massive laurels on the boundary provide a home for the equally impressive 9 m (30 ft)-tall 'Paul's Himalayan Musk' rose.

At the other end of the walk are two rectangular borders, in flower for most of the summer with a range of sun-loving herbaceous plants, including an interesting pink-variegated purple sage, teaming with the deep tones of a 'Garnet' penstemon.

From this point, the garden slopes uphill, planted much less formally with old apple trees, specimen trees and shrubs, and yet more old-fashioned roses. A striking feature of this part of the garden is the round 'beehive' thatched stone house, built by a local craftsman in the 1920s (although it looks much older) and now supporting a 'Schoolgirl' rose. Near by, and equally eye-catching, is a venerable ornamental cherry, with a show-stopping canopy of white, apple-blossom-like flowers in spring.

All gardens, even the best, have some disadvantages. According to Major Mordaunt-Hare, the sloping site creates a frost pocket in which many plants perish and the local wildlife can also be a problem. The Mordaunt-Hares used to grow soft fruit, but found they could not devise any form of protection from the squirrels. The mesh netting was disposed of in one night by a raiding party, whose teeth went through the replacement wire fruit cage with the ease of wire cutters. However, on the other side of the balance sheet, the garden is home to a pair of nightingales, and to hosts of bees and butterflies, drawn by the splendid collection of scented plants.

Climbing and rambling roses, left, flourish in this garden: Rosa 'Alexandre Girault' over an arch, and a massive 'Paul's Himalayan Musk', in the background.

Azaleas and forget-me-nots, right, create a splash of colour in spring reminiscent of an impressionist painting, set against the backdrop of a clipped beech hedge.

Gardener's Cottage

*An unusual, informal cottage garden, with some
delightful plant combinations and splendidly
eccentric garden sculptures*

VISITING THE Gardener's Cottage at West Dean bears a strong resemblance to Alice in Wonderland's journey down the rabbit hole. The cottage and garden are hidden away behind the nursery and gardens of West Dean College, where Ivan Hicks spends his working day. Not unnaturally for someone who is occupied with plants all day long, he views his garden as a place to relax; together with his wife Angie, he has created a magical small garden, designed to be used partly for their own pleasure and partly for the enjoyment of their two young children.

The garden itself is a relatively small square of land, but once you are through the gate into the garden you lose any idea of its size. The boundaries have completely disappeared in a thicket of plants, and the centre of the garden, in front of the cottage, has been given over to a circle of grass, rising in the centre to a grassy knoll topped with a sculpture. The Hickses have a great fondness for spirals, circles and organic forms. They clip the box into

spirals, an interesting touch of formality in an otherwise natural garden, and they also like using mirrors. Sculpture, visual tricks and jokes abound in the garden, many with allegorical or special allusions. But although the garden has something of the feel of a theatre set, the planting is the work of a master gardener, with a host of unusual and delightful plants, grown in part as the owners require and in part in sympathy with nature.

Their philosophy of gardening is to treat the garden as you would painting and sculpture; the topiary, arches, trees and shrubs provide the sculpture and the plants the painting. So often, says Ivan Hicks, people try to organize their gardens like a picture in a frame, but they put all the interest round the edge, rather than in the centre where it belongs.

The balance between artifice and nature, although it may appear to have just 'happened', has actually been thought about carefully. The blend of formality and informality, and of squares and circles, has produced a formal circular lawn in the centre,

*Visual jokes, like the one above, abound at
Gardener's Cottage. A pun on Magritte, this
glass head is filled with marguerites.*

*A dogwood (Cornus kousa), right,
underplanted with Cynara cardunculus, Rosa
'Cécile Brunner', viola, geranium and
Verbascum 'Arctic Summer'.*

A grassy knoll, *above, is surmounted by an arresting composition of a statue of the 'Green Man', with* Vitis vinifera *and nasturtiums entwining his ankles.*

Clipped box, *left, in the form of border edgings and topiary, provides a framework for planting that includes giant alliums, the huge leaves of the foxglove tree (*Paulownia tomentosa*) and the pink flowers of* Phuopsis stylosa.

A semi-circular *arch, right, is covered by the golden hop (*Humulus lupulus aureus*) on the left and the vine* Vitis coignetiae *on the right. Underneath, the glistening white foliage of ground-covering* Lamium *'White Nancy' glows out from the shade.*

The handsome foliage, *far right, and perfect sugar-pink flowers of* Rosa *'Gloire des Mousseuses', frames another of the Hickses' visual effects.*

edged with dwarf box and surrounded by the square of the enclosing walls, with the planting around the circle a satisfying mysterious jungle of plants and small, overgrown paths.

Among the plants you will find at Gardener's Cottage are a large number of old-fashioned and species roses, including *Rosa moyesii*, *R. rubrifolia* and 'Roseraie de l'Hay', while 'Gypsy Boy' and 'Albertine' grow into one other. The Hickses are particularly fond of *Rosa sericea pteracantha*, with its wonderful thorns and tiny flowers: it has to be coppiced to allow the thorns to be seen at their best. *Rosa* 'Kiftsgate', *Clematis montana* 'Tetrarose' and *Akebia quinata* mingle together on the cottage wall, with 'Kiftsgate', not unsurprisingly, winning the battle.

Tall dramatic perennials furnish the lower levels of the planting, with Miss Willmott's ghost (*Eryngium giganteum*), some self-seeding poppies and alliums, as well as lots of euphorbias and hardy geraniums among them.

To one side of the house is a tiny shaded garden, with a deep, mysterious water feature. The planting here is mainly evergreen and white, with ivies, ferns, hostas and white foxgloves, and *Thalictrum dipterocarpum* (syn. *T. delavayi*).

Just by the house wall is a huge and venerable yew tree in which the children have a tree house. Underneath, a campanula is trying to climb up the bole, surrounded by the silver-splashed and spotted leaves of pulmonaria and lamium.

Tiny paths, just wide enough to pass down, take you through and around the jungle of planting, allowing you to appreciate the scents and sights of the many exquisite plants that they have managed to cram into a very restricted space.

Owl Cottage

*A picture-postcard cottage garden, brimming with
old-fashioned roses, perennials and clematis,
surrounding an ancient thatched cottage*

VISITING Owl Cottage in the Isle of Wight in summer is rather like stepping into the pages of Beatrix Potter. Created and gardened by two sisters, Mrs Hutchinson and Miss Leaning, it is the cottage garden of everyone's childhood memories. A rich and wonderful profusion of delphiniums, roses, poppies, phlox and campanulas greets you as you come in through the garden gate, itself festooned with roses. The picture is framed by the thatched roof and thick walls of the ancient clunch-built cottage and the leaves and branches of an ornamental cherry, 'Pink Perfection', which offers its contribution in spring. Once the delphiniums are over, the starring role is taken up by a host of dahlias.

The plants are tightly packed in a rich mosaic of colour, which, although it has a plan and timetable, does not always perform to schedule. Whether or not the *Campanula lactiflora* will catch up with the delphiniums is always touch and go. A shocking-pink lychnis has seeded itself near the garden gate, in a vivid but

unscheduled patch of colour. The white form, which the sisters would prefer, cannot, apparently, be persuaded to grow in the garden.

In the border opposite the dahlias is a selection of Hybrid Tea roses, to which the bed was originally dedicated. Now a range of herbaceous plants grow up between them to prolong the flowering season, while some minature roses like 'Masquerade', 'Bush Baby' and 'Angela Rippon' line the path edge.

Scattered throughout the rest of the garden is a splendid selection of other roses, often grown with clematis scrambling over and through them. In one of the few attempts at formality, a line of 'Frensham' roses with their deep scarlet velvety flowers lines the path to the part of the garden behind the house. The delicious scent of the old-fashioned rose 'Madame Pierre Oger' fills this area in summer, but it really needs continuous dead heading, says Mrs Hutchinson. Behind the vegetable plot is a great blaze of mixed clematis, including 'Etoile Violette', 'Hagley Hybrid', 'Perle d'Azur' and 'Viticella Rubra'.

Argyranthemum *'Vancouver', above, is an
attractive pink marguerite, one of many
daisy-type plants that flourish in
coastal gardens.*

Old-fashioned *perennials, right, have been
planted at random. Here 'Shirley' poppies,
pink perennial verbena and* Campanula
persicifolia *'Alba' make a blaze of colour.*

Around the lawn to the side of the house, dominated by a massive weeping cherry, are the roses 'Fritz Nobis', 'Queen of Denmark' and 'Chaucer' with its pink sugar-candy blooms, an offspring of 'Constance Spry'. Other favourites are 'Buff Beauty' and 'Sarah van Fleet', which blooms all summer. Yet more clematis flourish here, usually entwined with roses or other shrubs, among them 'Lasurstern', 'Niobe' and 'Doctor Ruppel'.

The border close to the outbuildings is devoted to more unusual plants, including a range of butterfly antirrhinums in soft colours, and a green arum lily. Next to it is a bed of *Alstroemeria* Ligtu hybrids, all in soft art shades, which make a wonderful show in midsummer.

The sisters' general aim is to keep the garden as a typical cottage garden, with a continuous succession of flowers. The season starts with over twenty Japanese flowering cherry trees, which, along with the bulbs, provide a glorious spring display before the roses and clematis come into their own in summer.

CULTIVATION
Lavatera

LAVATERA is an excellent choice for providing height in a new, sunny border, because it grows fast and flowers over a long season. *Lavatera olbia* 'Barnsley' is one of the most popular. It is very vigorous (prune it hard after flowering) and grows head-high, with masses of pale pink flowers. *L. o.* 'Rosea' has deeper pink flowers and *L. trimestris* 'Silver Cup', an annual, rose-pink flowers.

The brilliant white daisy-like flowers of Osteospermum, *left, have an almost luminous quality when seen against the surrounding silver foliage.*

The deep herbaceous border, *far left, opposite the house, is dominated by* Lavatera 'Barnsley', *yellow day-lilies (*Hemerocallis*) and kniphofia.*

White Windows

A plantswoman's garden with
excellent contrasts of foliage form
and texture

I F ANYONE had told Mrs Sterndale-Bennett ten years ago that she would one day have a workable garden, she says she would not have believed them. The garden she inherited was nothing more than a long straight path, with reverted roses on either side, and vegetables at the end. She rose to the challenge of the blank canvas provided by a near empty and monotonously flat site and has created an informal country garden, with gently curving lawns and deep borders.

The colours in the garden tend to change with the seasons but the borders are, in fact, colour-themed – there are yellow, blue and silver, and red and pink ones, as well as a tapestry border and a variegated one. The borders have been created with shrubs and small trees at the back, to help divide the garden into distinct areas, and with tall perennials rising to meet the shrubs. One particularly good performer in this respect is *Eupatorium maculatum atropurpureum*, with its flat, rosy purple heads, which makes a good 1.8 m (6 ft) by autumn. Any odd gaps in the borders are furnished with annuals like tobacco plants and love-in-a-mist.

Now that the planting is in place, the skill, says Jane Sterndale-Bennett, is in keeping the shrubs in proportion, as there is a limit to how much you can prune them back. In any event, she likes the contrast provided by exuberant planting and neat lawn edges. Her borders are, none the less, meticulously kept and ruthlessly weeded. Showing visitors round the garden, she will dive on an errant forget-me-not, saying that she has never let one flower in the garden. Treated with the kindly discipline of a good nanny, the plants respond by looking singularly healthy and well-groomed.

Among the plants that do well in her garden are a large collection of euphorbias. *Euphorbia nicaeensis* is one of her favourites. Unlike so many of its untidier cousins, it has a compact habit, as well as sea-green foliage and attractive reddish stems.

The original dearth of trees has been corrected with several different forms of elder, including a *Sambucus nigra* 'Purpurea' (syn. *S.n.* 'Guincho Purple') with its deeply cut dark purple leaves and pinkish flowers, in striking contrast to a *Viburnum opulus* 'Aureum', the golden-leaved form of the guelder rose.

The silvery foliage, *above, of* Artemisia *'Valerie Finnis', and pale flowers of* Viola *'Moonlight' and the bright* Scabiosa *'Butterfly Blue' make an attractive combination.*

The general view, *right, shows how well foliage has been blended.* Phlomis russeliana, *in the foreground, is an excellent evergreen ground-covering perennial.*

A weeping crab apple now forms a focal point at one corner of the garden. Like all Mrs Sterndale-Bennett's trees, it was planted as a very young whip, which has apparently paid dividends. The temptation is always to buy big standards, but they then sit still for years, while the young whips overtake them.

Many of the plants at White Windows come from small specialist nurseries, although some are grown from seed. Jane Sterndale-Bennett is a member of the Hardy Plant Society and the National Council for the Conservation of Plants and Gardens, whose members swop plants, and she also keeps part of the national collection of hellebores. An entire bed is devoted to them in her garden, and includes several of the more unusual forms, such as *H.* × 'Nigercors' with its large cream flowers and *H. foetidus* 'Wester Flisk'.

At one end of the garden, screened from the house, is a bed devoted to hot colours, with *Euphorbia amygdaloides rubra*, and a *Photinia davidiana* 'Palette'. Equally well matched are *Silene dioica* 'Rosea Plena' and *Cimicifuga ramosa* 'Atropurpurea', which looks particularly dramatic on a dark day, with a columnar form of berberis, *B. thunbergii* 'Helmond Pillar'. *Pulmonaria saccharata argentea* also provides good foliage colour and form in the summer months, after flowering has finished.

Now that the planting is completed, the only problem facing Mrs Sterndale-Bennett is to find a home for the new and interesting plants where they will blend with the existing ones.

Interesting vistas, *left, are an essential ingredient of good garden design. Small trees, like the apple tree at the end of this border, act as a full-stop and screen other parts of the garden from view.*

Planning for height *in the border, right, is never as easy as it looks, since the plants rarely perform to a rule book. This green-and-gold scheme makes good use of contrasting foliage, including variegation.*

Hazelby House

A classic English country-house garden with splendid formal features and interesting plant combinations

WHEN MR AND MRS Martin Lane Fox bought Hazelby House some fifteen years ago, the house had been badly neglected and the gardens amounted to little more than a sloping lawn, a few rhododendrons and a ha-ha. Since then they have painstakingly created a classic English country-house garden with handsome stone terraces, formal walks, deep herbaceous borders, a rose garden, lily pond and ornamental lake. The first task was to create the basic framework of the garden, and the yew, beech and hornbeam hedges, which divide the different compartments of the garden, were planted. Since then the garden has evolved section by section, the newest element a woodland garden planted with azaleas, camellias and other acid-loving shrubs on the borders of the lake.

To the south side of the house is a large, open, paved terrace, with views down to the lake and to the rolling downland beyond. It has been planted with sun-loving plants in soft colours – white valerian, pale yellow tree lupins (*Lupinus arboreus*) and 'Hidcote' lavender included. A massive dome of *Rosa* 'Max Graf' makes a

focal point in the centre of the terrace, and clumps of *Stipa gigantea* catch the light with their glistening stems.

At the side of the house, past a handsome conservatory filled with the scent of regale lilies in summer, is the entrance to the rose garden. The formal arrangement of box-edged beds, enclosed by yew hedges, is softened by large numbers of shrub roses cascading over supports, with a thick underplanting of many unusual herbaceous plants and sub-shrubs. Among the roses is the moss rose 'William Lobb' with its exquisite mauve flowers like faded silk, and the Hybrid Musk 'Penelope', a mass of semi-double scented flowers. Other roses doing well are the dark reddish purple Gallica 'Tuscany Superb' and the Bourbon 'Reine Victoria', with its cup-shaped, richly fragrant, deep pink flowers. In the bed closest to the house, a mass of *Crambe cordifolia* looks particularly good at dusk, its huge leaves surmounted by clouds of white flowers.

Beyond the rose garden is the long walk, flanked by eighteenth- and nineteenth-century statues, backed by wide shrub and perennial borders. One of the best performers in this part of the

A lead statue, above, dating from the early nineteenth century, with the opulent 'Fantin-Latour' making a splendid foil for it.

A corner of the rose garden, right, with the large mauve heads of Allium christophii *in the foreground, surrounded by old-fashioned roses, in soft pinks, mauves and whites.*

In the white garden, *right, an eighteenth-century lead and stone sundial is framed by white roses, including 'Blanche Double de Coubert', with* Crambe cordifolia *and* Delphinium *'Mount Everest'.*

One of the many *exquisite planting combinations that abound at Hazelby House, right: the grey-green ribbed leaves of* Hosta fortunei, *with* Allium albopilosum *in front and* Rosa *'Belle Amour' behind.*

garden is *Abutilon vitifolium* 'Veronica Tennant' which is literally covered in lavender-blue flowers throughout early summer, while one of Mr Lane Fox's favourite roses, 'Fantin-Latour', with its delicate pink double flowers, makes a perfect foil for the statuary.

A gateway leads into a singularly well planted white garden, containing, among others, the silvery-white flowered *Geranium rectum* 'Album', white lychnis, more crambe, *Hosta* 'Thomas Hogg' (now correctly *H. undulata albomarginata*) with its creamy white flower spikes, *Veronicastrum virginicum album* and the heavily scented old-fashioned 'Mrs Sinkins' pinks.

The swimming pool beyond is effectively screened by a formal hedge of pleached limes, which are kept small by clipping three or four times a year. An unusual solution has been found for the normally rather untidy but attractive bronzy-orange flowered helianthemum 'Salmon Bee', which is being trained neatly up a

brick wall to great effect. Several quite tender plants do well in the shelter of the high brick wall in this part of the garden, including *Senecio leucostachys* (syn. *S. vira-vira*), and *Abutilon megapotamicum*, and *Wattakaka* (now *Dregea*) *sinensis*. Leading off from this area are the long main herbaceous borders backed with beech hedging, and with the central focal point of *Rosa* 'New Dawn' grown over a large white pergola.

The most recently created part of the garden is the area running down to the lake. Several rectangular shrub borders, like long fingers, point down to its margins, offset by the magnificent backdrop of the rolling countryside of the Berkshire Downs. The woodland garden beyond is still in its infancy, but with its Monet-style bridge over one end of the lake, and its collection of magnolias, eucryphias and azaleas, it looks set to become a major feature of the garden.

CULTIVATION
Phormium tenax

T HE EVERGREEN swordlike
leaves of *Phormium tenax*
(below) make it an ideal
subject for providing structure
in the border, or when grown
in pots. A variegated form, *P.t.*
'Veitchii' has cream-striped
leaves and *P.t.* 'Bronze Baby'
has reddish purple leaves.
Grow phormiums in a sunny,
sheltered site in light soil.
Protect in hard winters.

Vale End

A riverside cottage garden with herbaceous borders, an ornamental pond and fine views

IN A QUIET corner of Surrey, overlooking a fold of the River Tillingbourne, the gardens at Vale End have all the appeal of a traditional English country garden. In fact, although the Foulshams have been at Vale End for twenty-five years, it is only in the last ten that they have had time to concentrate on the garden. When they first came, there was little in the way of original planting, but they were fortunate in inheriting two large magnolias, including the lemon-scented purple form, known as *Magnolia liliiflora* 'Nigra', a large *Cornus mas* and some yews. Other trees, including a *Betula pendula* 'Dalecarlica', *Eucryphia* 'Nymansay' and the conifers, were planted by the present owners.

Springs in the garden feed the millpond below, and there are no less than four wells in the garden, which within living memory were used for the water supply. Much of the garden, as a result, is rarely short of water even in years of drought, which is just as well as the soil itself is a fairly free-draining sandy loam which would otherwise demand copious watering.

The border between house and terrace is planted in yellows and 'hot' colours, the colour scheme determined in part by the purchase of a 'Super Star' rose many years ago, one of Mrs Foulsham's first acquisitions. She says she is now rather astonished by her choice, but like all novices, she was drawn initially to the obvious big, bright plants. Subsequent years of practice and experience have altered her tastes but the 'Super Star' does its stuff admirably and she is reluctant to move it. Her only anxiety is that the long mauve racemes of the wisteria on the front of the house should be over before the rose starts to bloom. Variegated sisyrinchiums, Iceland poppies, senecios, rich purple-red berberis and a deep burnt-orange coloured helianthemum do well alongside the rose. Farther on, a combination of *Rosa* 'Madame Isaac Pereire' and *Clematis* 'Mrs Cholmondeley' grow on the house wall. The phuopsis in front of the dining-room window is another choice that Mrs Foulsham now laughs about – she realized, too late, that its strange foxy scent would drift in through the windows.

Iris sibirica *'Emperor', above, makes a vivid contrast with self-seeding poppies in a Monet-like combination, seen against the tiled roof of the house.*

The view *from the house, right, down to the River Tillingbourne. The bed in the foreground has a low profile, soft mounds of foliage contrasting with sword-like iris leaves and bright patches of flower-colour.*

CULTIVATION
Sisyrinchium striatum

THE TALL spires of creamy yellow flowers and iris-like slender leaves make a useful addition in midsummer to herbaceous planting in a sunny, well-drained border. Plant from autumn to spring, and cut off dead flowering stems in the late summer. Sisyrinchiums will often self-seed if the ground is left undisturbed.

Running down at right angles to the house is another deep herbaceous border, which is gradually being turned into a yellow and white one, with foliage plants and shrubs. Colour at the back comes from the brilliant golden leaves of the cut-leaved elder, _Sambucus racemosa_ 'Plumosa Aurea', coupled with the fluorescent foliage of a _Robinia pseudoacacia_ 'Frisia', while a full weeping standard 'Albéric Barbier' rose positively drips with little creamy yellow roses in summer.

Although the garden has a cottage-garden feel to it, small touches of formality have been introduced. Two yews back a small summerhouse that joins two borders within the shelter of the garden walls, and continuing Mrs Foulsham's fondness for standard roses, two 'Nozomi' roses stand sentinel at the garden gate. In spring the border at the entrance to the garden is a mass of scillas, lily-of-the-valley and hellebores, followed by a mixture of perennials and annuals in summer. Mrs Foulsham fills gaps in the border with large, dramatic annuals like cleome and _Nicotiana sylvestris_, and then biennials like _Digitalis lutea_ and the big, blowzy cup-and-saucer Canterbury bells, _Crambe cordifolia_ and peonies flesh out the perennial planting.

The small pond terraced into the bank on which the house stands is relatively new, fed by a natural stream. Around the margins of the pool are a brilliant mixture of salvias, dierama, hostas, cornflowers and self-seeding poppies (originally started from packets bought at Monet's garden at Giverny). In the cracks of the stone steps near by, the little daisy-like _Erigeron mucronatus_ (now _E. karvinskianus_) has seeded itself freely, as has love-in-a-mist in the neighbouring border.

Above the pond a small formal garden is in the making, its centrepiece a handsome pergola designed by Mr Foulsham, over which grows _Rosa_ 'Princesse Marie' with its delicate, pinky white flowers. In the bed near by, sedums, hydrangeas, artemisias and _Lavatera olbia_ 'Barnsley' flourish, while a golden-leaved hop spreads itself over the wall.

Behind the house, a small white-painted courtyard glows with colour in summer, principally from hardy fuchsias, petunias and everlasting erysimum. Houseleeks make fascinating hummocks on the tiles of the outhouse roof, while one end wall of the courtyard is almost covered by the huge leaves of _Vitis coignetiae_.

Future plans include ecological planting on land running along the top of the garden, and, down by the millpond, marginal plants like iris and giant gunnera are being introduced.

The small formal pool, _left,_ _with_ Aubrieta _'Red Carpet' in the_ _foreground,_ Polygonum bistorta _'Superbum' behind, white_ Anthemis cupaniana _and the gold_ _grassy leaves of_ Carex elata _'Aurea' beyond._

The handsome _large leaves,_ _above, of the umbrella plant_ (Peltiphyllum peltatum) _at the_ _foot of a small wall. It needs_ _moist soil, but will grow happily_ _in sun or shade and makes an_ _excellent poolside plant._

17 Fulham Park Gardens

A tiny formal walled garden with an elegant planting scheme in silver, green and white

ASTUTE garden writers have long been urging town dwellers to create formal gardens on their pocket-handkerchief sized plots, and Anthony Noel's garden in Fulham proves their point. It is a gem of a garden, just three years old, tucked behind a typical turn-of-the-century terraced house, and opened for the first time for the National Gardens Scheme in 1990.

An actor before he turned garden designer, Anthony Noel has used his sense of theatre to great advantage in the garden. The sculptural effects of clipped box, the enclosing brick walls and the York stone surrounding the tiny square of brilliant green turf make a splendid backdrop for an exquisite collection of largely white and silver plants, with a few blacks and purples thrown in for dramatic contrast.

His meticulous attention to detail is another reason why the garden works so well. He has laid the small brick courtyard leading into the garden so that you would be hard pressed to know that it did not actually date from the same period as the house. By using old bricks and by deliberately making the surface very slightly irregular and uneven, Anthony Noel has succeeded in making it appear old and naturally worn.

Every square centimetre of ground and wall has been used to advantage, and a raised bed at the end of the garden helps to add plant interest at different heights, as do the flowering climbers. A white wisteria and several forms of clematis grace the walls, including 'Etoile Violette' (bought as 'Gravetye Beauty' – yet another instance of careless nursery labelling), 'Nellie Moser' and 'Royal Velours'. He is particularly pleased with the wonderful clematis 'Alba Luxurians', with its green-and-white striped flowers – 'like a living version of Regency silk'. Equally unusual and worth having is the *Cobaea scandens*, a half-hardy climber with sweet-pea-like leaves and bell-shaped flowers throughout the summer.

Tightly packed into the borders is a splendid collection of silver and white plants including the dramatic, though tender, *Melianthus major*, lots of different achilleas and artemisias, a

Stone sculpture of a girl's head, above, crowned by the ivy-leaved geranium 'L'Elegante', and half-hidden by the leaves of Rosa *'Madame Alfred Carrière', which has creamy white flowers.*

Cool evergreens, like clipped box, right, and ivy, make an excellent foil for a changing display of flowers. In summer the terracotta pots are planted with petunias; in spring, with tulips.

•SOUTH EAST•

A lion's-head mask, *centre, surmounted by the golden-leaved hop,* Humulus lupulus aureus, *trickles water on to an arrangement of pebbles, flanked by neatly clipped balls of box* (Buxus sempervirens).

A terracotta urn, *right, filled with Danish marguerites and* Helichrysum petiolare, *is set off by the handsome large dark leaves of the Canary Island ivy,* Hedera canariensis *'Gloire de Marengo'. In the foreground are the elegant flower spikes of* Hosta sieboldiana *'Elegans', the large blue-grey leaves of which make excellent ground cover in semi-shade.*

silver-leaved lavender (*Lavandula pedunculata*), *Helianthemum umbellatum* 'Wisley White', *Verbascum elegantissimum* 'Mont Blanc' and a 'White Pearl' valerian.

Like many small-garden owners, Anthony Noel makes use of attractive terracotta pots for short-term displays. The black-and-white pansies in winter give way to black tulips in spring, and white petunias in summer. His black-and-white theme is echoed in the permanent planting of black aquilegias with a cream-and-white striped form of Solomon's seal, and white peonies.

A trellis arch, *above, supports* Clematis *'Nellie Moser', with its carmine-striped pale pink flowers. It flourishes on a cool, shady wall, making it an ideal subject for town gardens where light is often restricted by neighbouring houses.*

Field Farm

A medium-sized garden, with a
wonderful selection of roses, in the
heart of the High Weald of Kent

ROSES – in particular old-fashioned roses – are Mrs Gault's passion. At Field Farm, they grow in chaotic profusion, over pergolas, up walls and in hedges. Compare a photograph of Field Farm as it was, its only plant a single holly tree swamped by a vast sea of grass, with the richness of the planting today, and you begin to understand what creating a garden really means.

One of the first things the Gaults did was to make a screen of fruit trees, grown espalier-fashion on wooden poles, round the house. The 1.8 m (6 ft)-wide brick path leading from the barn and garage up to the house was already there, but it has now been softened by planting twin pergolas on either side, over which scrambles a mass of rambling roses. Planted originally in pairs on either side of the path, they now embrace one another to make a gloriously unruly hedge. Among them are: 'Ballerina' with its apple-blossom-like sprays of pink-tinged white flowers, the Hybrid Musks 'Penelope', 'Felicia' and Moonlight', the Bourbon 'Zéphirine Drouhin' and the ever-popular 'Albéric Barbier', with its tight creamy buds opening to white flowers.

Pink and white roses, above, are often found in partnership at Field Farm. Here, deep pink 'Zéphirine Drouhin' and creamy 'Stanwell Perpetual' scramble over a pillar.

On the barn at the foot of the brick path is a massive rose, *R. brunonii* 'La Mortola', which has almost covered the wall in the three years it has been there. It sends out huge shoots rather like 'Kiftsgate', and may well have been happier climbing a tree. Near by is the species rose *R. californica* 'Plena' which Mrs Gault first saw at Sissinghurst. The more open, wild-looking roses give her great pleasure. As she points out, once hooked on roses, it is hard to stop planting them and she now has more than ninety-eight different kinds.

Growing up under the roses are hardy geraniums, foxgloves and clouds of catmint (*Nepeta mussinii*), the dusky foliage and feathery blue flowers an inspired foil for the soft pinks and creams of the roses. Planted under the espaliered fruit trees, 'James Grieve' alternating with 'Worcester Pearmain', are tulips, species daffodils and scillas, which look spectacular in spring with the apple blossom. Planted thickly in layers, they give a long season in a relatively small area of soil.

Tucked behind and to one side of the barn is the swimming pool, a pot-pourri planting of honeysuckle, roses, philadelphus

Large bushes, right, of Rosa 'Nevada' with its creamy flowers and R. 'Marguerite Hilling', underplanted with Geranium endressii, almost screen the house from view.

and a pineapple-scented Moroccan broom (*Cytisus battandieri*). Making an informal hedge to one side of the pool are 'Erfurt', the Rugosa 'Fru Dagmar Hastrup' with its single carnation-pink flowers and wonderful hips in autumn, and the Gallica 'Charles de Mills', its tightly petalled maroon flowers fading off to purple.

Although the roses flourish in the deep clay soil, planting them was no easy matter. The holes had to be dug with a pickaxe, and the infill soil was collected by wheelbarrow from the various molehills in the surrounding fields.

To one side of the house there is a small sunken garden in stone and brick. When it was first dug, it filled up with water and the Gaults' friends assumed they were making a pond. The plants have now taken over the sunken garden for themselves, in a colour scheme of soft pinks, mauves and whites, the seat almost covered by the pink *Cistus × purpureus*.

Behind the house the colour scheme changes to yellows, blues and purples. The roses here are mainly modern shrub ones, including 'Frühlingsgold' with its golden semi-double scented flowers early in the year and 'Frühlingsmorgen' with clear pink and yellow single flowers. 'Golden Wings' is another favourite rose, with its single pale yellow blooms.

Steps then take you up to an enclosed garden with a mown path through wild flowers to a seat where you can sit and watch the sunset. To one side, a long curving hornbeam hedge hides the area containing a tennis court from the rest of the garden; beyond it is a small ornamental potager, its centrepiece a terracotta pot with trailing nasturtiums, with the radishes, lettuces, carrots and cabbages in orderly formation below.

***Yet more roses**, left, in the foreground. This time Rosa Mundi and the apothecary's rose (*Rosa gallica officinalis*) with* Lavandula stoechas *and* aquilegias *beneath. In the background is* Spiraea japonica *'Goldflame'.*

Rosa *'Pink Bells', above, in the foreground, underplanted with the silvery woolly leaves of* ballota. *The climber 'Golden Showers' adorns the back of the house, flowering continuously until the autumn.*

Bates Green Farm

Recently created plantsman's garden with spectacular herbaceous borders planted for year-round colour, woodland garden and rockery

ALTHOUGH THE gardens at Bates Green Farm extend for more than an acre, it is the magnificent herbaceous borders, planted only recently in what was once the vegetable garden, that Mrs McCutchan is, justly, most proud of. She has opted for a subtle blend of colours, moving from soft, deep bluish reds at its deepest to light silvers and yellows, through mauves, pinks and blues, with some attractive and unusual combinations, in terms both of leaf and flower colour, and of plant shapes. Among the most successful groups at the deep red end of the border are *Rosa* 'Magenta', *Campanula latiloba* 'Hidcote Amethyst', red fat hen (*Atriplex hortensis* 'Rubra') – a self-elected member of the group – dark red lupins, and the wine-coloured leaves of *Berberis thunbergii atropurpurea*.

The border is planned to have colour all year round, although it is obviously more sparse in winter and at its most impressive in the summer months.

Her own favourite groups in the border are the silver, blue and pale yellow combinations, in particular the azure blue of *Salvia*

haematodes and *Geranium pratense* 'Plenum Caeruleum'. *Salvia sclarea turkestanica*, evening primroses, assorted silver-leaved thistles, verbascums and delphiniums provide height in the borders, along with old-fashioned roses and an attractive silver-leaved *Elaeagnus commutata*, while poppies, geraniums, campanulas and phlox provide the lower levels with colour.

Of the other combinations, *Lychnis coronaria oculata*, with its pink and white flowers, looks good with the art shades of the 'Fairy Wings' poppies and the silver leaves of eryngium, while *Clematis* 'Etoile Violette' makes a perfect match with the soft mauve flower spires of *Buddleja alternifolia*. A bower set into one of the borders is adorned with *Clematis* 'Niobe' and 'Rouge Cardinal', backed up by rich, dark magenta gladioli and asters, and old-fashioned sweet peas.

Beyond this garden room lies a small, newly planted woodland garden, filled with spring flowers – late narcissi, colchicums and species crocus – and shade-loving plants, like hellebores, ligularias, rodgersias and peltiphyllum, foxgloves and pulmonarias.

The rockery, above, in the front garden, with a range of green and gold dwarf conifers and hummock-forming plants.

The flower garden, right, with Hesperis matronalis alba *in the foreground, backed by phlox, lupins and poppies, with giant thistles behind.*

The brilliant scarlet *papery flowers of 'Goliath', above, a cultivar of* Papaver orientale, *mingling with the tiny blue flowers of* Borago officinalis.

Upper Mill Cottage

Large country garden, divided into garden 'rooms', with a profusion of old-fashioned roses

BUBBLING through the centre of the gardens is the millstream from which the cottage takes its name. It now provides a haven for all kinds of wildfowl, as well as the trout which Mr and Mrs Seeney feed rather than catch. The flora seem to enjoy the conditions as much as the fauna obviously do, and Upper Mill Cottage boasts a rich and varied collection of plants in a picture-postcard setting. Like all keen collectors, the Seeneys are constantly battling with their desire to find space for new plants, without destroying the balance of the existing planting.

When they bought the cottage some nineteen years ago, there was little or nothing to preserve, apart from the ruined mill buildings, which were only revealed when the covering carpet of ivy and old man's beard was rolled back. The structure of the garden, down to the dry stone walls of Kent ragstone, has been created by the current owners. They have tried by and large to be governed by what will grow well in the conditions, and as the garden is fed by a large number of springs, which tend to pop up unexpectedly in different parts of the garden, they are luckier

than most in the range of plants they can grow.

In the shady, damp areas near the former mill, a wide range of water-loving plants flourish, including many different forms of mimulus, primulas and the blue meconopsis, as well as ligularias and rodgersias, and a curiosity, *Actaea pachypoda* (syn. *A. alba*), the fruits of which closely resemble eyes on organ stops. The mimulus tend to cross-pollinate so that you get many different shades, from the palest to the darkest. On the banks of the stream, in the centre part of the garden, there are Himalayan cowslips (*Primula florindae*) and Tibetan cowslips (*P. sikkimensis*), *Iris sibirica*, which is grown from seed in pale blue, white and dark blue forms, and various lobelias, including the dark red *L. cardinalis* and the paler 'Pink Flamingo'. Also doing well here are *Nepeta govaniana* with its lemony smell, blue and white camassias and a variety of astilbes. Toad lilies (*Tricyrtis macropoda* and *T. ohsumiensis*) and an attractive small clover with blackish purple leaves (*Trifolium* 'Purpurascens Quadrifolium') – known as Calvary, because it was reputed to have grown under the Cross – all add subtle touches. *Senecio smithii*, gunneras and

The rich blue flowers, above, of Meconopsis betonicifolia 'Harlow Carr Strain' with Ligularia dentata 'Desdemona' behind, flourishing in moist conditions near the stream.

In a shady corner of the garden, right, Iris sibirica puts on a good display, backed by the huge leaves of Gunnera manicata. The ground cover is Vinca minor 'Argenteovariegata'.

An informal archway, *below, of* Laburnum × watereri *'Vossii'* *and weeping green and copper beeches. The plants leading up to the archway are* Stephanandra incisa *and* Symphoricarpos orbiculatus.

the massive leaves of lysichiton grow by the water's edge, as do several different forms of fern.

Under the nearby willow is a shady bed filled with ground-cover plants, like hostas, pulmonarias, vincas, comfrey and London pride, planted in large drifts, which make a peaceful counterpoint to the more vivid borders of herbaceous perennials. The hostas under the willow are seldom eaten by slugs, and the Seeneys now believe that the bits of bark that drop on the leaves act as some kind of deterrent. They are testing out the theory by shredding bark themselves and using it as a slug deterrent on ligularias, in the hope that they have found an ecologically sound way of getting rid of slug damage.

Near the willow is a pretty dawn redwood (*Metasequoia glyptostroboides*), the leaves of which turn a delightful shade of pink before they fall, and the fresh growth in spring is an attractive lime green. As the Seeneys point out, it is not a tree for a small garden – it has reached 9 m (30 ft) in nine years and may well one day reach 45 m (150 ft). They have planted a good range of trees, a number of which they have grown from seed, including a *Ginkgo biloba*, a catalpa and a horse chestnut. One of the best shrubs, they think, is the Carolina allspice (*Calycanthus floridus*), which is very hardy. It has oval aromatic dark green leaves and fragrant brownish red flowers, with masses of spreading petals, from early to midsummer.

To keep the cottage feel of the garden, the Seeneys go in for what they term 'jungle planting', with layers of plants coming out one after the other, and for contrasts in foliage colour and texture. They also allow the plants, where appropriate, to climb through and over each other: a climbing aconite, for example, is being trained through a winter honeysuckle, while *Rosa* 'Guinée' scales an old 'Edward' apple tree, once popular as a pollinator but now quite rare. The perennials in the borders are planted because they enjoy the conditions rather than to fit in with some pre-ordained colour scheme, which the Seeneys feel would look contrived in such an informal garden. They also use a wide range of geraniums as border fillers, including the attractive double form, *G. grandiflorum* (syn. *himalayense*) 'Plenum', the familiar 'Johnson's Blue' and the sprawling pink carpet of *G. sanguineum lancastrense* (syn. *G.s. striatum*). There are also many forms of lobelia and salvia, including *Lobelia laxiflora angustifolia* and *L. tupa* and *Salvia candelabra*, and the unusual almost black-flowered *S. discolor* from Peru, as well as a wide range of old-fashioned and species roses, which are, apparently, much less trouble than the modern ones. The Seeneys are particularly fond of the moss rose 'Chapeau de Napoléon' (syn. *R.* × *centifolia* 'Cristata'), the aromatic mossy buds of which are harvested for pot-pourri, although the blooms too have a glorious scent. Other favourites are the dark red 'Souvenir du Doctor Jamain', the nearest thing there is to a black rose, which is set off at Upper Mill Cottage by the white 'Moonlight' rose planted near by.

In a small patch of acid soil at the top of the garden, the Seeneys have created a woodland garden, where they find to their delight that they can grow things that would perish elsewhere in the garden. Hellebores, including 'Purple Chalice' and 'Picotee White', do well here, as do yellow *Meconopsis regia* poppies. The red, blue, white and multicoloured pulmonarias in a new bed in the garden look singularly healthy, forming large-leaved clumps. Mr Seeney attributes their well-being to the fact that after flowering he cuts them down to the base – a tip well worth copying in one's own garden.

Ground cover, *right, in the shade of a large willow is provided by* Vinca minor *and mixed hostas. In the foreground, the white flowers of* Cosmos bipinnatus *'Purity' gleam out above a froth of London pride* (Saxifraga × urbium).

Elsing Hall

Romantic medieval moated house and gardens
with old fashioned roses, wild-flower meadows and
a sweeping orchid lawn

THE MEDIEVAL moated manor of Elsing lies in the heart of the Norfolk countryside, and its magnificent tall chimney stacks (in fact ingenious nineteenth-century imitations) are first glimpsed from the narrow oak-lined lanes. Elsing Hall was built in about 1460 by the Hastings family, and passed through the female line into the twentieth century. In 1958 the family sold it, and thereafter the house and garden became sadly neglected until it was fortunately rescued by David and Shirley Cargill in 1982.

A tree-lined drive sweeps around to the imposing north front and takes you across a small bridge over the moat, whose walls are covered with roses and clematis. On one side a golden hop entwines itself through *Rosa* 'Francis E. Lester', late Dutch honeysuckle and *Clematis tangutica*. The garden completely surrounds the manor, and almost every view and aspect contains large, still expanses of water and delicious reflections.

The arched front door of the house is framed by two towering clumps of the giant hogweed *Heracleum mantegazzianum* – a bold way of softening the austere knapped flint walls. On the south side of the house there is a paved seating area. Here borders of old-fashioned roses, philadelphus and pinks, together with such architectural plants as euphorbias, senecios and phlomis, separate the terrace from the moat. The steps down to the water are a delightful tumble of valerian, feverfew and the little daisy, *Erigeron karvinskianus* (syn. *E. mucronatus*), also known as 'daisy-gone-crazy'. No paving or gravel is allowed to show if a plant, however humble, offers itself.

When Mr and Mrs Cargill bought the derelict manor there was one lawn, which had been mown like a bowling green. Gradually Mrs Cargill noticed some spotted leaves and stopped mowing whereupon a sea of the most beautiful orchids appeared. This lawn had probably been cut for thirty or forty years, but the

The drive up to the imposing front entrance of the manor, above, with a golden-leaved hop on the right twining through Rosa *'Francis E. Lester'.*

The Gothic façade, right, of Elsing Hall seen from across the moat. Borders of old-fashioned roses separate the terrace in front of the house from the water.

orchids had never given up. They have now been joined by many other wild flowers and fritillaries.

Looking back at the house you can admire the wide variety of climbing plants covering the flint walls. Roses 'Madame Grégoire Staechelin' and 'William Lobb', with its dark purple blooms like old silk, tower over *Paeonia delavayi lutea*, and 'Madame Alfred Carrière' scrambles up the gable. Across the moat the planting concentrates on large-leaved plants, with groups of rheums, rodgersias, gunnera and peltiphyllum.

To the east of the house lies the old walled vegetable garden. When the Cargills moved here you could not get through the door. So they cut and burnt, and battled with the bindweed. Having cleared the brambles and nettles, they decided to use the magnificent brick walls and ancient fruit trees as hosts to more of their favourite roses and climbers. In the warmest spot a Tibetan clematis, with attractive ferny leaves, flourishes beside a Banksian rose. An unidentified creamy double rose was discovered sprawling on the ground and full of suckers, and now grows happily with *Rosa* 'Anemone' and *Lonicera sempervirens*.

An area which has recently been cleared surrounds an old stew pond, dredged like the moat. Planting here is relatively new, but primulas and irises, followed by phlomis, cistus and ribes, are growing well after a good mulching with mushroom compost.

Another area under development is the formal parterre with a hornbeam hedge, low lavender and box hedging and clipped box balls. A newly planted ginkgo avenue leads back towards the moat and a winter garden planted in 1986 with winter-flowering plants and colourful berries.

The path around the moat continues past interesting modern sculptures, across a small bridge. A new collection of willows, maples, cherries and birches forms an arboretum, with a variety of foliage and coloured bark. The planting at Elsing Hall is generous and ebullient, but without ostentation, and all the plants are in harmony with the spirit of the place.

The view from the house, right, over the wild-flower lawn, now a haven for orchids and fritillaries as well as the more everyday meadow flowers.

The front terrace, right, with an attractive tangle of gravel planting, including architectural clumps of Euphorbia characias wulfenii *and alliums, with self-seeding pinks, valerian and feathery fennel, as well as old-fashioned roses.*

Magnolia House

Small completely walled village garden, with mixed borders, hardy and tender plants, and an ornamental pool

MARK RUMARY has had years of experience in designing gardens for other people, and has put his wealth of knowledge to good effect in his own garden. Magnolia House is an old timber-framed house on the main street of Yoxford, modernized by the Georgians and re-antiqued by the Edwardians. The garden seems larger than half an acre, as it is cleverly laid out to make the best possible use of the space. It is also enveloped completely by magnificent old walls, in some places 3.5 m (12 ft) high. These walls plays host to a huge variety of climbing plants, such as wisterias, clematis, roses and honeysuckles.

An ancient mulberry of unusual height and spread casts its shade over the centre of the garden, which is divided into 'rooms', each with its own character and atmosphere. Through a yew arch is a Moorish garden where a raised pool is surrounded by Mediterranean flowers and exotic plants in pots. The almost evergreen rose 'Albéric Barbier' is reflected in the cool water, where koi carp, some twelve years old, glide among the water lilies. Two

borders, punctuated by exclamation marks of clipped box, are planted with spring bulbs, followed by well-chosen plants including campanulas, *Romneya coulteri*, alstroemerias and drifts of *Allium christophii*.

Beyond another yew hedge, garlanded with scarlet *Tropaeolum speciosum*, lies a small garden where only white-flowering plants are allowed. A circular lawn embraces an elegant white-painted urn, surrounded by a bed of white begonias.

Pleached limes are planted against the road to keep the noise down, and a bench has been positioned to give a long view of the garden. Beside the bench *Philadelphus* × *lemoinei* is grown for its perfume. Many of the plants are chosen for their sweet smell, and scents of roses, philadelphus and honeysuckle mingle and linger in the still air.

Mark Rumary believes that a garden should have some interest all the year. In this formal structured garden he aims to compose deliberate 'pictures' for the summer and autumn, and to depend on individual plant interest in winter and early spring.

The delicate pale pink flowers, above, of Rosa 'Max Graf' combine perfectly with the large starry heads of Allium christophii.

The raised pool, right, backed by a clipped beech hedge. The leaves of Iris pseudacorus 'Variegata' make a feature in the foreground.

Park Farm

Cottage-style plantsman's garden
with a wide range of plants for
shade, sun and water

THE DAY that Jill Cowley signed the contract for Park Farm and the two acres around it, its old barn fell down. Seeing the garden created on its site, with its luxuriant blend of old-fashioned roses, herbaceous plants and self-sown seedlings, it is hard to believe it was a pile of old bricks and timbers only eleven years ago; but presumably underneath the rubble and old beams lay tons of wonderful manure, the product of four hundred years of continuous cattle farming.

The garden surrounds a delightful white-painted house which has been rebuilt and added to over and over again since the original construction was completed in 1342. A central chimney stack was added in 1810 to Gothicize it. Park Farm was the home farm for the Elizabethan house, Langleys, near by, and became its *ferme ornée*.

Glimpsed through the proliferation of plants lie the softly rolling pastures of the Essex countryside and the gently mooing cows. There is an atmosphere of tranquillity in the garden itself, with the donkey braying and the bees buzzing around the hive. Beds brim over with euphorbias, senecio, sisyrinchium, feverfew

and *Alchemilla mollis*, and hidden among the alchemilla are pots of white petunias. The creams, pale yellows and greens are suddenly brightened by a clump of dark blue *Iris sibirica*.

The garden is imaginatively divided into different theme 'rooms', and architectural features designed by Derek Bracey give structure and formality where needed. The Chinese garden is shaded by a temple tree (*Sophora japonica*) and a paulownia, grown from a seed brought back from the Villa Taranto in Italy. 'Duchesse de Nemours' and 'Sarah Bernhardt' peonies are mulched regularly with the donkey Benjamin's manure, a service he has provided for twenty-three years. Jill Cowley's only wish is that he would provide lots more.

Bold statements are made by a huge clump of the biennial sage, *Salvia sclarea turkestanica*, and in one bed by a mass of *Crambe cordifolia*, seven or eight years old, which tumbles across the paths. Beyond is the garden of the giants, where heracleum towers over gunnera, rheums and rodgersias.

Jill Cowley likes the garden to look comfortable and furnished, even in winter. This is achieved by planting box and yew hedges,

The head of Neptune, above, by the pond, with Vitis *'Brant'* and variegated ivy above, and ostrich plume ferns (Matteuccia struthiopteris) to the left.

Rosa 'Complicata' scales an old apple tree, right, framing the view of the Victorian dairy. 'Trier', the massive Pemberton Musk rose on the left, flowers non-stop.

In the garden *of the giants, right, as it is affectionately called, huge heads of* Heracleum mantegazzianum *in front of* Petasites japonicus, *a yellow elder and a stand of* Salix exigua *make a dramatic combination, interplanted with hostas, rodgersias and irises.*

A tiny daisy *from Mexico,* Erigeron karvinskianus, *below, together with red and white valerian (*Centranthus ruber*), softens a flight of steps made from old kerb stones.*

and with a white bench secluded between an elegant pair of *Chamaecyparis lawsoniana* 'Green Pillar'. Vistas are used to draw your eye towards the surrounding fields, and to make the view almost integral to the garden by providing another level of contrast.

A myriad old-fashioned roses climb and ramble over every available tree and support. One favourite is *Rosa* 'Alba Semiplena', a wonderfully simple rose with bright yellow stamens and lovely leaves. Mrs Cowley admits to growing roses mainly for their names, and adores the 'Holy Rose of Abyssinia' (*R. richardii*), believed to have been found in the tombs of the Pharaohs in the pyramids and in Minoan tombs. 'Rambling Rector' and 'Blushing Lucy' share a bed, and 'Albertine', 'Complicata', 'Madame Plantier' and a few wild roses fight to reach the top of one old apple tree.

Under a fifty-year-old walnut tree mahonias, hellebores, snowdrops and aconites thrive in the winter garden. There is a garden with hot colours, and a 'Roman' ruin on the old barn foundations. In the 'arid garden' cats hide under a foamy cut-leaved elder to fish the goldfish out of the canal.

Memories of Tolstoy and Russian picnics are created by the pale trunks of a group of birches in long grass. Near the small herb garden, bordered by box and pretty blue *Phacelia campanularia*, Mrs Cowley has planted a 'chalk garden', despite the fact that their soil is basically heavy Essex clay.

You can step out on to a tall wooden platform, soon to be covered by *Vitis coignetiae*, to admire the pond and the little moorhen house. A plan is afoot to terrace the bank on the other side of the pond, as it is difficult to maintain and work on.

A charming Victorian dairy, built in 1810 in Gothic style, in which the milkmaids boiled and scalded away, is now used on open days for serving tea and cakes, which are laid out on pink and white china on the large kitchen table.

Waterside giants

THERE are some fine architectural-looking plants that thrive in damp conditions, including *Heracleum mantegazzianum*, which grows to about 2.4m (8ft), with large rough divided leaves, up to 90cm (3ft) across, and umbels of white flowers in late summer. *Gunnera manicata* has even bigger leaves – sometimes up to 1.5m (5ft) across – and conical light green flower spikes in summer. The crowns need protection in winter, otherwise the young leaves may be damaged by frost. *Rheum palmatum*, an ornamental rhubarb, is rather smaller, with similarly divided leaves, but is very wide-spreading; the leaves are flushed red when they first appear.

Wyken Hall

*Formal country garden with a range
of planting styles, including knot,
rose, herb and woodland gardens*

THE WYKEN HALL estate has been in the same family since 1920, but the latest developments to the garden under the present owners Kenneth Carlisle and his American wife Carla began in 1978. The Carlisles have been ably assisted by John Mann, a skilled and enthusiastic gardener who started working at Wyken in 1946.

The old seventeenth-century farmhouse was enlarged in 1920, and has recently been decorated in a striking coppery limewash. Surrounding the house are various gardens designed to create different moods and styles. A number of yew and box hedges have been planted over the last few years which, as they mature, will help to give more structure and shape to the garden.

In order to make the approach to the house less severe the Carlisles designed a line of espaliered apples, shrub borders and a quincunx. This is a slightly adapted version of a design created by Gertrude Jekyll for Knebworth, and consists of five interlocking circles in brick and Suffolk flint. The four outer circles have wedding cake topiary in yew in the centre, surrounded by spring bulbs preceding ornamental cabbages. A simple pond and fountain are planned for the central circle of the quincunx.

A new gate leads into the east garden, where a 'red hot' border featuring yellow, flame-red and orange flowering plants is being created. Beyond this lies the kitchen garden, ultimately to be designed as a French potager, with espaliered fruit trees and an arbour at the end.

The brick area behind the house is divided by yew hedges into three sections, with a herb garden at one end and a knot garden at the other. This was designed by Arabella Lennox-Boyd after a weekend visit in 1984, to replace a hotchpotch of beds and paths. A Gothic seat painted a grey-blue presides over the herb garden. *Magnolia grandiflora* shows off its handsome creamy flowers, and *Carpenteria californica* its beautiful white blooms, rather like a generous rock rose. Two weeping white mulberries accentuate the knot garden, which is at its best in early summer with irises, peonies and lavenders.

In 1978 a doorway was knocked through the wall to an old orchard, and a rose garden was created for old-fashioned roses.

In the rose garden, above, Rosa 'Complicata' makes a magnificent arching bush, covered in pale pink single flowers in midsummer.

A place to rest, right, and absorb the sights and sounds of the knot garden. Clipped evergreens flank the seat, while the climbing rose 'Dortmund' scales the wall behind.

Looking across the rose garden, left, towards the pergola with alliums and several different geraniums, including 'Johnson's Blue' and 'Kashmir White', and Libertia formosa.

The central sundial, left, in the herb garden, surrounded by golden marjoram and thrift, with an edging of chives. Roses, including the Gallica 'Charles de Mills' with its fragrant deep magenta flowers and the pink-flowered 'Félicité Parmentier', create the hedge behind.

Delphiniums and foxgloves peer up through roses such as, among others, 'Fantin-Latour', 'Maiden's Blush', 'Boule de Neige' and 'Hebe's Lip'. A long wooden pergola, inspired by one on the canal terrace at Bodnant, is covered in white and blue wisteria, clematis, roses and honeysuckle.

The Carlisles regret the lack of water in their garden, and, as well as the project for a quincunx pool, plan to replace an urn with a low Gothic fountain in the centre of the rose garden. More ambitious plans include a pond beyond the rose garden gate, to be surrounded by rushes and lilies, and to reflect the sky beyond.

An ancient English oak presides over a dell where wild flowers are nurtured. Cowslips, primroses and daffodils thrive, but the fritillaries are usually nipped off by gourmet pheasants overnight. A row of silvery *Salix elaeagnos* (formerly *S. rosmarinifolia*) has been planted to screen the area from the open country.

A new avenue of lime trees was planted in memory of Mr Carlisle's father who loved Wyken, and on either side of a pair of gates stand two pillars designed to echo the chimneys of the house. The slates on the gates were beautifully worked by the doyen of English carving, David Kindersley. The gates and avenue draw your eye towards the trees beyond, and join the garden to the woods.

A woodland garden was cleared of scrub and planted in 1983. Embedded in a stone seat is a shell three million years old, dug up from a crag of the Pliocene age during excavations for a Suffolk bypass. The view from this seat is towards a winter garden. Kenneth Carlisle particularly enjoys this area, which was one of his first attempts at garden design. He likes the way in which it is concealed and goes to sleep in the summer. Hellebores fill the beds, and early irises, tulips, daffodils and scillas rise bravely from the paving. Winter jasmine, mahonias and sarcococca are grown for their sweet scents. *Viburnum farreri*, *Cornus mas* and the golden elaeagnus all add colour to this winter garden, which is at its best in the bleak months of January, February and March.

Brook Cottage

Large country garden on a steeply sloping site, with a wealth of interesting plants, and carefully linked but very different planting styles

TUCKED INTO a valley at the end of a narrow lane, Brook Cottage is an attractive seventeenth-century house. Set all around it on steeply sloping land is a remarkable garden, first started twenty-five years ago by the current owners, Mr and Mrs David Hodges. It encompasses an astonishingly wide range of different design and planting schemes which the Hodges have linked together, and to the surrounding, ever-visible landscape, with great skill.

As a visitor to the garden, you are directed round its four-acre expanse in a carefully organized route, which enables you to appreciate each area of the planting as it was intended to be seen. As you pass through the gateway from the forecourt, you are assailed, in early summer, by the pineapple scent of the golden flowers of a large *Cytisus battandieri* on your right, and, on the left, by the sight and scent of the anemone-like white flowers of *Carpenteria californica*. Stretching in front of you is a terrace enclosed on two sides by stone walls that shelter many of the less hardy plants in the garden and on the other two sides by clipped yew hedges.

The garden is full of hidden springs, and when the lawn beyond the terrace was levelled an overflow from the natural supply to the house was diverted to form a channel round the lawn. This now makes an effective division between the lawn and the bank, the latter surmounted by an impressive avenue of flowering 'Shirotae' cherries (*Prunus* 'Mount Fuji'). The bank itself is faced with rough slabs of local ironstone, and the planting of predominantly foliage plants and flowering shrubs, with moisture-loving plants near the water, has adapted over the years to the increasing shade as the cherry trees above have extended their canopy.

Below, in the valley bottom, is the large water garden – a sinuous sheet of water balanced effectively by architectural planting, with pampas grass, gunnera and silver-leaved cardoons forming

Simplified planting schemes, above, often make the greatest impact. Here the Floribunda rose 'Apricot Nectar' has been teamed with Iris pallida *'Variegata', the foliage of which is attractively striped.*

A border near the house, right, with bush roses, including 'Doris Tysterman' with orangy red flowers and 'Congratulations' with double pink ones, underplanted with catmint, and backed by Rugosa roses.

one massive group, contrasting with single specimens of the Kilmarnock willow (*Salix caprea pendula*) and the splendid evergreen bamboo, *Chusquea culeou.*

Most water gardens, attractive though they are, create problems of one sort or another, and at Brook Cottage they had to contend with damage from voles, who were turning the water into their private leisure park. Mr and Mrs Hodges commissioned a specially designed (and humane) trap, which proved surprisingly successful, and once the unharmed prisoners were moved to new quarters upstream, they presented no further problems. Nearer to the brook itself, planted for its winter stem colour, is *Rubus cockburnianus*, with its glistening white stems, and its more civilized but less spectacular cousin, *R. thibetanus*, as well as various equally attractive forms of willow and dogwood.

A tunnel formed by copper beech hedges leads into an enclosure where a path of stepping stones winds upwards between moisture-loving plants like arums, astilbes, primulas and *Iris sibirica*. Beyond the tunnel is an acre of grassland, blending into the surrounding fields, which has been planted with a range of handsome trees and flowering shrubs, including more than 120 different shrub roses. Towards the boundary, viburnums and cotoneasters cover the sloping ground, and in the damp area by the brook are balsam poplars and the handsome willow *Salix elaeagnos* (syn. *S. rosmarinifolia*) with its attractively spiky foliage.

Turning back past the tennis court, the path is flanked on one side by a bank, with a blaze of mixed helianthemums in summer spilling over a low stone wall, while the netting of the tennis

***The large pond**, left, that was created from a boggy corner of a former field. It is now thickly planted with, among others,* Carex stricta *'Bowles' Golden'* (in the foreground), water lilies *and* Iris laevigata *in the pool, and* Primula florindae, Hemerocallis *and the creamy spires of* Aruncus sylvestris *behind.*

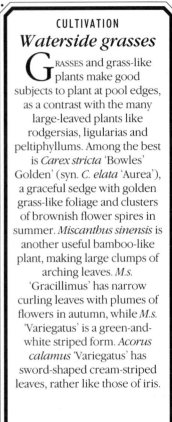

CULTIVATION
Waterside grasses

GRASSES and grass-like plants make good subjects to plant at pool edges, as a contrast with the many large-leaved plants like rodgersias, ligularias and peltiphyllums. Among the best is *Carex stricta* 'Bowles' Golden' (syn. *C. elata* 'Aurea'), a graceful sedge with golden grass-like foliage and clusters of brownish flower spires in summer. *Miscanthus sinensis* is another useful bamboo-like plant, making large clumps of arching leaves. *M.s.* 'Gracillimus' has narrow curling leaves with plumes of flowers in autumn, while *M.s.* 'Variegatus' is a green-and-white striped form. *Acorus calamus* 'Variegatus' has sword-shaped cream-striped leaves, rather like those of iris.

*A **silver-leaved** pear, above, combines with the dark red flowers of a rose, underplanted with alliums, rue and foxgloves.*

court on the other side supports some attractive clematis, including 'Huldine', its single white flowers making an inspired contrast with the tulip-like deep red flowers of 'Gravetye Beauty'.

Forming a focal point connecting the different levels is a large pond, thickly margined with moisture-loving plants, including large-leaved hostas, ligularias and euphorbia, and invaded by the determined spread of *Iris laevigata*. From here the way leads past the avenue of cherries to the top of the garden, where herbaceous planting predominates. Below the high stone wall, which supports many tall shrubs (including the rarely seen silver-leaved *Buddleja farreri*) and climbers, are a peony bed and a mixed shrub and herbaceous border.

Interesting foliage contrasts are a feature of the garden, and below the house this is amply demonstrated by the dark yellow domes of *Hebe ochracea* combined with the stiff blue grass *Helictotrichon sempervirens*, and the feathery trails and bright yellow flowers of *Tropaeolum polyphyllum* with the neat dark foliage of *Berberis corallina* 'Compacta'.

In front of the house, set against a dark yew hedge, is an extremely well-planned white border, which looks good right through the summer until early autumn. Two columns of white clematis, and the tall shrubs *Philadelphus* 'Virginal', *Deutzia scabra* 'Candidissima' and *Spiraea nipponica* 'Snowmound' rise above a gleaming sea of white valerian, white delphiniums, silver artemisias and other white perennials.

A nearby pink and blue border has also been carefully orchestrated to give contrasts of height and form. *Prunus* 'Spire' and two clematis intertwining on an iron support provide the verticals, while *Lavatera olbia* 'Barnsley', *Galega orientalis*, penstemons, phlox and polemoniums make the middle band, with low-growing plants like diascia, origanum, festuca and geraniums carpeting the ground.

*A **massive cotoneaster**, left, sprawls over the steps leading from the courtyard behind the house to the herbaceous borders beyond. Rosa 'Bobbie James' dominates an old apple tree on the left, underplanted with fuchsias and edged with silvery* Artemisia splendens.

Cecily Hill House

*Town garden with herbaceous
borders, good shade planting and
an attractive small potager*

ANY OF THE garden owners in the National Gardens Scheme can relate daunting experiences of clearing waist-high undergrowth before they could start work planning their gardens. Cecily Hill House can go one better: during World War II, when the Army requisitioned the house, they used the garden as hard standing for tanks. Although this was well before Mr and Mrs de Zoete's time, some of the concrete remains not far below the surface, limiting the scope for major changes to the layout.

The garden had, in fact, been very well planted by the two previous owners when the de Zoetes took it over about twelve years ago, and they inherited some handsome mature trees and a number of good roses. The de Zoetes' principal contribution has been to divide the garden into compartments, and give it a structure that it lacked, as well as adding some interesting new plants of their own.

Among the plants they inherited and which help to establish the garden's framework is a magnificent *Viburnum davidii*, forming a huge evergreen dome covered in spring with pinkish flowers

and later with attractive metallic blue berries. The trees that came with the garden include a large weeping ash and several ornamental cherries, chosen well, according to Mr de Zoete, so that they provide a continuous display of blossom in spring, first pink and then white, as well as the delicate winter flowers of *Prunus × subhirtella* 'Autumnalis'.

The borders that surround the garden, enclosed by stone walls, have been planted with an eye for foliage as well as flower colour. The dark magenta leaves of *Heuchera micrantha* 'Palace Purple' make a good contrast with the silver foliage of *Artemisia* 'Powis Castle' and *Stachys byzantina* (originally from Beth Chatto's nursery in Essex). The silvery blue, pink and purple colour scheme is continued with different forms of salvia, alliums and geraniums, plus *Penstemon* 'Sour Grapes', the attractive Michaelmas daisy *Aster × frikartii* 'Mönch' (also from Beth Chatto) and the whorlflower, *Morina longifolia*, with its evergreen spiny foliage and whitish pink summer flowers, which came from Rosemary Verey's garden just up the road from Cecily Hill House. In return, Mrs Verey has taken seed

Lilium *'Sterling Star', above, grown in large terracotta jars in the courtyard, makes a spectacular display in summer, combined with others like 'Mont Blanc' and* L. *regale.*

The ornamental cherries, *right, immediately behind the house put on their spring show. The shade here is used for pulmonarias, hostas and ferns.*

from one of the de Zoetes' favourite plants, the soft strawberry-coloured foxglove _Digitalis_ × _mertonensis_, which they propagate very successfully.

A shady part of the border near the house makes an ideal place for several different hostas, including _H. sieboldiana_ 'Frances Williams' (much loved by the slugs) and _H.s._ 'Elegans', as well as tiarella, heuchera, epimediums, astrantia, filipendula and brunnera – they have a particularly good form, _B. macrophylla_ 'Variegata' (syn. _B.m._ 'Dawson's White'), with creamy white borders to the heart-shaped leaves, and small delicate blue flowers in spring. There are a number of different ivies and ferns, including the crested buckler fern (_Dryopteris_ Cristata group), which does well in the moist soil.

The arch and screen between the courtyard and the main garden were designed by Mr de Zoete. Weathered now to a subtle deep sea-green, it provides support for several old-fashioned roses, including 'Félicité Perpétue' and 'Compassion'.

In the potager, screened by neatly clipped yew hedges, and with clipped box balls and four standard gooseberry bushes emphasizing its formal design, the de Zoetes grow mainly herbs – lovage, applemint, fennel and so on – as well as decorative red and green lettuces in an oval pattern.

In the gravelled courtyard to the side of the house the de Zoetes have made a collection of some particularly handsome pots, several of them old acid jars. These now house collections of lilies – such as 'Sterling Star', 'Mont Blanc', 'Connecticut King' and _Lilium regale_, whose intoxicating scent fills this part of the garden in summer – as well as irises, pelargoniums and an impressively large and venerable hosta.

At the front of the house, blending with the soft golden Cotswold stone of the handsome early eighteenth-century façade, are architectural clumps of euphorbia, vying with Jerusalem sage (_Phlomis fruticosa_), St John's wort and artemisias for the lion's share of the pavement.

**The shaded border**, left, beyond the potager, with its handsome eighteenth-century lead tank, complete with gently trickling water spout. The lush, large-leaved perennials here include hostas and brunnera. There are also two good scented shrubs for semi-shade, Mahonia _'Charity' and_ Choisya ternata.

**The ornamental potager**, left, screened behind a yew hedge, has one bed devoted to neat circles of red and green Italian lettuces. Clipped box balls marking the corners of the beds and standard gooseberries (not shown) provide architectural interest.

40 Osler Road

*Mediterranean-style semi-formal town garden
with many exotic plants and some inspiring
design features*

THE MOST satisfying gardens usually have a disciplined core, fleshed out with an exuberant and carefully chosen planting scheme. The gardens at 40 Osler Road are no exception, but what makes them particularly interesting is that they are right in the middle of suburban Oxford, and the Cootes have not only spent a great deal of time and energy researching and planning the basic framework of the garden, but they also grow a range of exotic plants.

Set in about two-thirds of an acre, and hidden from the road by a high wall, the gardens surround the house on three sides. The Mediterranean-style architecture of the house, coupled with the Cootes' love of classical Italian gardens, has had a considerable influence on the design.

The centrepiece of the garden, set in front of the drawing-room windows, is a formal lawned rectangle, enclosed on three sides by clipped yew hedges, fronted by rectangular box-edged beds containing massed plantings of lavender, santolina and sedum

respectively. At two corners are raised stone pots of trailing silvery-leaved helichrysum, pelargoniums and lobelia, in shades of white, pink, magenta and blue. In the centre is an octagon of clipped box, infilled with glistening white dimorphotheca (*Osteospermum ecklonis*) and surmounted by a Chusan palm. Linking the drawing room to this part of the garden is a wide brick-paved terrace which the Cootes fill in summer with exotic plants in pots, including a pair of magnificent *Datura* (now *Brugmansia*) *versicolor* 'Grand Marnier' whose huge buff-apricot heads of tubular flowers drench the terrace with their scent. Oleanders, shrubby salvias and echiums, plus an olive tree in a terracotta pot, all contribute to the Mediterranean feel of the terrace.

The inspiration for the formal garden came from the Riviera garden of La Garoupe, with its parterres of santolina, rosemary and lavender. The sedums were an inspired substitute for the rosemary, their rosettes of leaves and flat heads of flowers giving them a sculptural appearance, rather like a woodcut.

The centrepiece of the front courtyard, above, is a handsome Phoenix canariensis *in a large oil jar, surrounded by a sea of 'Whirlygig' nasturtiums.*

A corner of the formal garden, right, where a pot of Helichrysum petiolare *and pelargoniums ('Blue Fox' and 'Bird's Egg') rises above beds of sedum and santolina.*

A further reference to the Italian landscape has been created with a grass walk behind the yew hedges, lined with Irish junipers (*Juniperus communis* 'Hibernica'), a hardy smaller-scale substitute for Italian cypresses.

At one end of the grass walk is a grassed mount, surrounded by a double octagon of lonicera hedges and topped with a further cube of hedging, making a container for an exotic shrub in a pot (inspired by the Villa Lante). It makes an interesting geometric feature and a vantage point from which to look over the low yew hedges of the formal garden to the lush planting beyond.

Leading from the mount back towards the house is another grass walk with a shrub border on one side, edged with clipped mahonias to give shelter from the wind, and two parterres on the other. The Cootes realized that if you are busy working during the day, your best opportunity to view the garden may well be when you get up in the morning. This is a modern application of

CULTIVATION
Datura

THESE exotic-looking plants, now known as *Brugmansia*, with huge trumpet-shaped flowers come mainly from Central and South America. They are generally frost-tender and the shrubby species need greenhouse treatment in winter.
They need light, fertile soil and plenty of water in the growing season. *D. versicolor* (below) grows to around 6m (20ft).

In the small shady clearing in one corner of the garden is a collection of stone monkeys, seen in spring, right, with a blaze of bluebells, and in late summer, far right, when the large leaves of Tetrapanax papyriferus *have emerged.*

The exotic trumpet-shaped *flowers, left, in the left of the picture belong to* Datura *(now* Brugmansia) versicolor *'Rosea'. Below, a mixture of silvery-leaved plants including* Malva sylvestris *and* Sidalcea *'Elsie Heugh' are echoed by the silver-leaved pear, through which climbs* Clematis viticella *'Purpurea Plena Elegans'.*

**Junipers**, left, lean drunkenly along the grass walk on the right of the picture. In the border on the left are Ceanothus 'Perle Rose', Lythrum salicaria 'The Beacon', Anemone tomentosa _and_ Acanthus spinosus. _Crowning the mount at the end of the walk is the handsome large-leaved exotic_ Musschia wollastonii.

**Leading from** the formal garden, left, to the more exotic area, a grass path is lined on one side with the yellow flowers of Hypericum 'Hidcote' _and on the other with the spiky needles of_ Pinus strobus 'Nana' _and_ Berberis dictyophylla.

the _piano nobile_ of the Italian villa, in that the garden should look satisfying when viewed from above. The formal garden and the parterres to one side of it were created with that in mind. The principal element of the knot shape is created by many cherry laurels, with a centre of golden lonicera, and a fringing of argyranthemums and white dahlias.

Beyond the parterre and in front of the kitchen window, the Cootes have created a herb garden, surrounded by an unusual variegated 'hedge on stilts', as Mrs Coote describes it, created by _Acer platanoides_ 'Drummondii', planted at close intervals and with clear stems to about 2 m (7 ft). The variegated leaves give the impression of golden sunshine, in contrast with the dark green mass of a clipped yew and the boundary trees beyond.

A narrow passage leads through to the front courtyard, which has been turned into a Mediterranean dry garden, with a long and wide gravelled drive and a turning circle in the front of the house. A feathery-leaved _Genista aetnensis_, rising above clusters of pots of colourful annuals and exotics, acts as a focal point in one corner, and euphorbias and hydrangeas border the house.

Leading away from the house, to one side of the formal garden, is a grass path lined with herbaceous and shrub borders, with a number of exotic plants. Thanks to the free-draining soil, some overwinter in open ground, _Acacia pravissima_, eriobotrya, colletia, and _Salvia guaranitica_ among them. The Cootes have concentrated here on architectural plants and on glaucous foliage. _Melianthus major_ and _Ricinus gibsonii_ mingle their magnificent foliage in one bed, while a huge _Yucca recurvifolia_ dominates the opposite bed.

The design has emphasized the axes of a relatively small site to provide interesting vistas at various points and to invite exploration at others. For example, concealed around a distant corner, strange stone monsters rear up among ruined pillars and evocative foliage. It is supposed to suggest the ephemerality of human endeavour, although one young visitor simply called it 'spooky'!

The Old Rectory

Large country garden with a rose garden,
herbaceous borders, a man-made pool and a large,
beautifully designed potager

THE PLANTING at the Old Rectory has the understated classic appeal of an English country garden, although Mrs Huntington, who has been largely responsible for the planning and planting, is in fact an American. She was born and brought up in upstate New York, where her gardening experience was largely limited to the rhododendrons and azaleas that thrived in the naturally acid soil and woodland character of the region.

In the six years that the Huntingtons have lived at the Old Rectory, they have gradually altered and improved the garden, section by section. The existing circular rose garden was originally planted in much smaller segments and contained roses of all varieties and colours. It has been redesigned using softly blending pinks and mauves from David Austin's new named varieties. There are twelve different ones, including 'Mary Rose', 'Claire Rose', 'Chaucer', 'Admired Miranda' and 'Wife of Bath'. The edging has been planted with *Nepeta* × faassenii.

Lilium *'Mont Blanc', above, is one of several different lilies grown in the herbaceous borders at the Old Rectory, many of which are deliciously fragrant as well as beautiful.*

Two herbaceous borders have been made on either side of a great sweep of lawn, with a well-established cedar as its focal point. Below these borders runs a stream, together with a new pond, backed by pollarded willows and several rare forms of *Betula* and *Arundinaria*, and an adjacent bog garden.

The making of the pond was carried out by Mr Huntington, who hired a JCB to dig it out, and then lined it with plastic, covered by felt carpet underlay, with soil on top. It has provided the perfect environment for great swathes of *Butomus umbellatus*, its rushy leaves and pink umbrellas of flowers providing welcome cover for the fish, which would otherwise almost certainly have been snatched by marauding herons.

Leading from the pond towards the potager are four borders divided by grass walks. They are planted with old-fashioned perennials such as tree lupins, delphiniums, peonies, foxgloves, alliums and thistles, including a particularly attractive one with metallic blue heads, *Eryngium* × *zabelii* 'Violetta'.

The rose circle, *right, now replanted with David Austin roses in soft mauves, whites and pinks. In the distance is the ornamental pear,* Pyrus salicifolia.

A different theme, above, in one of the borders, with the accent on foliage interest from Artemisia *'Powis Castle'*, Miscanthus sinensis *'Gracillimus'*, Molinia caerulea *'Variegata'*, the dark leaves of Heuchera *'Palace Purple'* and Acanthus spinosus.

The large potager, far right, is a masterpiece of geometric planning. Marrow, clematis and vines climb the iron tunnel running through the central axis, apples and pears are grown on espaliers and the vegetable beds are neatly edged in lavender, chives or hyssop. Roses are grown both as standards and trained over arches.

The long border, right, where Lilium *'La Rêve'* combines very successfully with the David Austin rose 'Ellen'.

The handsome large potager beyond was laid out a few years ago to a traditional design of mixed vegetables and flowers, and was created with the help of Rosemary Verey. Neat brick paths create the compartments in the potager, with espaliered pear trees, step-over apples and box edging providing the framework and clipped box balls and spirals marking the corners. In the centre a pergola creates a focal point, covered with *Rosa* 'Félicité Perpétue' and *Clematis* 'Marie Boisselot'. Standard roses give height to the beds and add a nice decorative touch.

Higher up the garden, what was once a wilderness to one side of the house has been transformed into a woodland garden, which is particularly pretty in spring, when the massed planting of narcissi, crocus and cyclamen holds sway.

A steep north-facing bank at the front of the house has been put to good use for mainly shade-loving plants, and is planted with epimediums, erythroniums, trilliums and daphnes, as well as variegated ivies and maples, like *Acer davidii* 'George Forrest'.

Turn End

Large town garden with many interesting
compartments, and a range of plants for different
conditions, from shady woodland to hot dry sun

THE GARDENS at Turn End are impressively well maintained, but some twenty-seven years ago, when the Aldingtons designed and built the house at Turn End, they were more like a jungle. The land had belonged to a Victorian house next door, and had lain neglected for years. When they tried to survey it, the undergrowth was so thick they had to make a tunnel to stretch a rope across, and then twang the rope to find the person at the other end.

Underneath it all, though, there were the remains of a garden, with old apple trees, and primroses, bluebells, daffodils and ivy below, which the Aldingtons decided to leave (in the part near the house) in a more or less natural state. They have added ground cover in the form of *Vinca minor* and *V. major* 'Variegata' and now dead-head the bluebells to prevent them taking over. They have also added several roses, including 'Frühlingsgold', *Rosa rubrifolia* (*R. glanca*), and down the path, a *Rosa webbiana*, with all the delicacy of the wild dog rose but a longer season, and 'Cerise Bouquet', which is threatening to take over. A small grove of birch trees has been added close to the house, including *Betula alba septentrionalis* (planted as a whip) and a *Betula utilis jacquemontii* (planted as a standard). The whip has won, proving the adage that it pays to plant trees young.

A gravel path round the edge of this area reveals self-seeding onopordums, foxgloves, a sprawling carpet of the pink-flowered *Geranium sanguineum lancastrense* (syn. *G. s. striatum*), monkshood, and pulmonarias, epimediums, violets and cyclamen. A weeping forsythia (*F. suspensa*) is doing so well that a tunnel has to be made with secateurs to allow room to walk under it. More delicate than the standard forsythias, it also looks much more at home in its woodland setting than it would if planted with Kanzan cherries and Leylandii cypresses, the unfortunate combination so often seen in suburban gardens.

Beyond the woodland garden, the view opens out on to a grass glade which curves through the garden, providing its central

The archway, above, with the rose 'Félicité Perpétue' adorning it, a collection of containers forming the centrepiece, and the yellow horned poppy in the foreground.

A giant thistle (Onopordum acanthium), right, on the right of the picture and Iris 'Smoky Dream' frame a view of the less formal area of the garden.

The tiny courtyard, *above, next to the house, where the water hawthorn (*Aponogeton distachyos*) with its distinctive waxy white flowers flourishes in the shady pool beneath a giant* Robinia pseudoacacia.

core. In spring the borders on either side are full of bulbs, followed by irises, which do particularly well. The Aldingtons have counted fifty-seven heads on one large clump. The first border is colour-themed in blues, pinks and reds, with a large range of herbaceous perennials, backed by artichokes and tall thistles.

A huge chestnut tree in the lawn, towards the far end, marks a natural dividing line, and beyond it is a yellow, white and silver border, with yellow-barked cornus, the golden-flowered tree peony (*Paeonia delavayi ludlowii*), artemisia, poached-egg flowers (*Limnanthes douglasii*), yellow foxgloves and an attractive yellow deadnettle (*Lamium maculatum* 'Aureum'), as well as golden variegated lemon balm and imperial fritillaries. A white 'Dairy Maid' rose and the white climber *R. helenae* provide height at the back of the border. To the north side of the house are two shady borders, devoted largely to different hellebores, white ones in one bed, and pinky reds in the other.

A beech hedge divides this part of the garden from the formal area beyond, the land and outbuildings having been acquired at a later date. One part has been turned into a sunken garden, with an octagonal brick patio, the planting inspired by John Brookes and filled with daisies, at their best in late summer. The other is a formal parterre, edged in box and paved with old stable bricks. In spring, the infill planting of wallflowers makes a rich contrast with the bright blue flowers of the aptly named *Ceanothus* 'Cascade' which has taken over the high wall enclosing one side of the garden.

At the opposite end of the garden, reached through a small arch from the woodland garden, are two sun-filled enclosed gardens. The smaller of the two is in Mediterranean style, with a large antique terracotta oil jar as a focal point, and with roses and honeysuckles covering the walls. The larger has been divided into four raised beds planted with a profusion of sun-loving plants,

The giant allium (Allium christophii), *left, in the fore-ground, backed by a spectacular display from the rose 'Cerise Bouquet' overhanging the path.*

A magnificent terracotta pot, above, by Monica Young, flanked by ferns and foxgloves in the woodland garden.

The coach-house*, below, frames the view of the box-edged parterre, seen from the octagonal daisy garden. A Cordyline australis in a container creates the focal point, underplanted with the glistening white Osteospermum ecklonis.*

with a handsome flowering cherry as the focal point, and a long pergola covered with roses, clematis and vines making a very attractive backdrop.

A further arch leads into a small courtyard contained by the house, shadowed by a large acacia, where a pool laps against the house, cleverly designed with only a sheet of glass between the pool and the living rooms. As water lilies do not grow in the shade, Mr Aldington has introduced water hawthorn to the pool, whose elegant long leaves lie flat on the water, while the waxy white heads of its flowers are raised, water-lily-like, aloft.

In spring the small copse of silver birches near the house, left, comes to life with hundreds of bulbs, including tulips and bluebells, with mixed wallflowers fringing the lawn. The handsome large leaves in the foreground are those of the ornamental rhubarb, Rheum palmatum.

The parterre behind the coach-house, right, is filled with wallflowers in spring, followed by lobelia in summer. Peter Aldington has used stable bricks to pave the paths, their dark tones providing a neat counterpoint to the brilliant flower colour.

CULTIVATION
Parterres

Geometrically organized beds, edged with neatly clipped foliage plants and filled with either gravel or a disciplined, simplified planting scheme, have long been a feature of classical European gardens. In a small space, it pays to keep the scheme as unified as possible, with a single colour theme, or with a single species used for the infilling. Trained standards make ideal centrepieces, as do handsome large-leaved plants, like yuccas, phormiums or palms, in a raised pot. The paths and the edgings must be meticulously maintained; for the former, brick, gravel or granite setts are ideal (or stable bricks, as at Turn End) and for the latter santolina and lavender can be used instead of box.

Herterton House

Beautifully designed and planted garden with three distinct areas: a formal front garden, a physic garden and an exquisite walled flower garden

THE GARDENS at Herterton House are divided into three self-contained sections, each with a different planting scheme: a formal winter garden at the front of the house, a herb garden at the side and a flower garden at the back. Beyond the latter are the nursery and stock areas from which the Lawleys earn their living.

When the Lawleys took over the house fifteen years ago, the buildings had been adandoned and the area that is now the garden was a mass of rubble and weeds. Their plantsmanship, together with their enthusiasm for garden history, have combined to create one of the most interesting gardens in the North of England.

At the front of the house, on a slim rectangle of land, they have created a formal, predominantly evergreen, winter garden. Winter is, after all, the longest season in this part of the world, sometimes continuing for more than half the year. In its formality, overlooking as it does the natural Northumbrian landscape, the garden provides a neat contrast with the ideas of 'Capability' Brown, born only four miles away from Hartington. As Frank Lawley points out, 'Capability' Brown's work seems to have involved a remaking of the Northumbrian landscape over the rest of Britain; and from the formal garden at Herterton House you look out over the classic ingredients of his landscapes – gently rolling hills, a twist of water and clumps of trees.

The principal framework of the winter garden is made up of bays of tightly clipped box (*Buxus sempervirens*), now standing about 90 cm (3 ft) high, but originally bought as tiny plants, and a parterre of four squares, edged with *B. s.* 'Suffruticosa', with a central pyramid of golden box (*B. japonicus* 'Aureus'). It is now hard to believe that fifteen years ago the plants, then tiny cuttings, all fitted into the Lawleys' Renault 4. The other principal evergreen structure plants are ivy, yew and holly, with variegated

The lower parterre, above, at the front of the house, with dwarf box (Buxus sempervirens *'Suffruticosa'*) edging and domes of golden Japanese box framing the view.

The physic garden, right, with green cotton lavender, variegated mugwort and Galega *'Lady Wilson'*, a mauve and white form, prominent in the deep border.

and gold-leaved forms providing year-round colour and interest in the garden.

Between the box bays and the parterre is a magnificent thyme bank. Created from *Thymus* 'Aureus', a more or less non-flowering form, it adds its delicious fruity smell to this part of the garden. Round the doorway to the house the Lawleys are patiently growing a box porch: the two plants, either side of the door, have taken twelve years to reach half-way to their final destination – the top of a canopy over the door. In the heavy snowfalls that are a winter feature in this part of the world, they are often flattened to the ground, only to spring up with great fortitude with the thaw.

Round the corner of the building is the herb garden, or physic garden as the Lawleys have now learned to call it, enclosed on two sides by buildings and on the other two by stone walls. No larger than 9 m (30 ft) or so square, it has been designed as a knot garden, with small beds edged with miniature London pride set 'posy-fashion' around the central bed, which features a large silver-leaved pear (*Pyrus salicifolia*), clipped twice a year into a formal shape. The large deep border down the south side of the herb garden has been designated for aromatics, among them hyssop, sages and meadowsweets (the latter was Queen Elizabeth I's favourite strewing herb).

In summer the herb garden is also rich with the scent of old-fashioned roses, the variegated Rosa Mundi (*R. gallica* 'Versicolor'), the old black rose of Tuscany and three different Alba roses. Burnet roses flank the arches (known as 'eyes' in Northumbria) to the old granary, and these are clipped as tight as box after they have flowered – an attractive alternative if you want the formality of box with the bonus of flowers.

Behind the arches of the granary, which give the garden the air of a medieval cloister, is a paved area with a seat, backed by two

The orange bed, left, one of the centre beds in the flower garden: behind the ancient font in the foreground are Lilium bulbiferum croceum *and* Helenium 'Moerheim Beauty' *with* Alstroemeria aurea 'Dover Orange' *on the right. On the wall behind is the old Glory rose 'Gloire de Dijon'.*

*The centrepiece of the knot garden, left, is the weeping silver pear, surrounded by a bed of silver periwinkle (*Vinca minor 'Argenteovariegata'). *The surrounding beds are edged with dwarf London pride, and in the foreground are herb marigold (*Calendula officinalis*), vervain (*Verbena officinalis*) and summer woodruff (*Asperula tinctoria*).*

seventeenth-century statues which originally adorned the battlements of nearby Alnwick Castle, having been presented by a former Duke to local freemen when he refurbished his castle.

From the herb garden, you turn the corner into the walled flower garden, a brilliant virtuoso display of perennial flowers in formal themed beds, surrounded by raked sand paths. Originally it was planted in random fashion, until the Lawleys realized that it needed the framework of a colour theme to restrain its exuberance. With the determination that only dedicated gardeners can display, they took everything out of every single bed and re-arranged it in a colour scheme that follows the progression of the sun, with the pale 'dawn' colours near the house, moving towards the strong 'midday' colours in the centre, and the deep rich colours of 'sunset' farthest from the house.

The sources of the plants are widespread, with a concentration of native British plants, many from Northumbrian gardens (among them a local painter's garden, planted up in the 1930s), and a 'treasury of old plants', according to Frank Lawley.

Among the groups of plants that flourish in this part of the garden are a great range of campanulas in the 'midday' beds, where the rich orange of lilies, heleniums and alstroemerias contrasts with the strong blues of adjacent beds. Among the many campanulas are local harebells and a rare cup-and-saucer form that Frank Lawley found in a ditch, and has managed to propagate and sell through the nursery for the last three years.

Near the house, in the 'dawn' beds, is a frothy mixture of gypsophilas and achilleas, including the Lawleys' own white form with grey leaves, 'Hartington White', which originated as a

CULTIVATION
Eryngium giganteum

THE BIENNIAL sea holly (*Eryngium*) is commonly known as 'Miss Willmott's Ghost' (after the keen but eccentric Edwardian gardener who strewed seeds of it in other people's gardens). With its tall blue flowers, and silvery spiny bracts, it makes a good back-of-the-border plant for sunny situations. Plant from seed in autumn.

The panorama *from the flower garden, right, with old helenium hybrids and* Achillea *'Moonshine' in the foreground.*

Looking north *in the flower garden, far right, with* Phlox maculata *'Alba' and* Artemisia *'Silver Queen' in the foreground.*

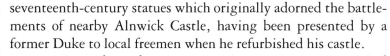

seedling in the garden, and an attractive and unusual pink cow parsley. At the far end, in the 'sunset' beds, are the deep red flowers of astrantia, cape figwort, alliums, phuopsis and sedums, penstemons ('Garnet' and 'Firebird'), irises and aquilegias.

The long borders, running down either side of the formal flower beds, have a gold-and-green theme, and are largely devoted to shrubs. The Glory rose 'Gloire de Dijon' on the west-facing wall makes a toning backdrop with its pinky buff flowers.

In a more formal area close to the house, evergreens have been used for permanent planting, in particular ferns and hollies. Otherwise, in this part of the garden, there is very little to see until early summer, when the sun climbs back above the house and the glowing tapestry of colour makes its reappearance.

Bank House

Informal plantsman's seaside garden with trees, shrubs and perennials for shade and sun

CLOSE ENOUGH to Morecambe Bay to bear the brunt of the salt-laden winds that sweep in from the sea, Bank House nevertheless manages to play host to some fascinating plants, many of them from South America. Seeing the garden today, with its sweep of immaculate emerald-green turf and well-kept beds of perennials, it takes a leap of the imagination to visualize it as it was when Mr and Mrs McBurnie took it over a good many years ago. Their early years in the garden were spent cutting down head-high nettles and removing the farming debris that lay neglected on the land. Like all good gardeners, they have been remodelling and renewing parts of the garden ever since.

At the far end of the garden, backing on to the canal, they have planted a small arboretum 'for their old age'. At the moment the trees, principally poplars, alders, birches and rowans, are planted in small copses in the grass – which still needs cutting – but the plan is that they will ultimately grow and create a small, more or less maintenance-free woodland. Not yet problem-free, they had

some trouble with mice harvesting the hazel nuts, and put wire netting round the boles to stop them. Unfortunately, the mice – far from being deterred – used the netting like an adventure playground.

Between the woodland area and the house is the vegetable garden, where besides the usual vegetables, Mr McBurnie grows his own tobacco. After harvesting, it is strung up to dry and then sent to to a tobacco cooperative to be turned into dried leaf tobacco.

Next to the vegetable garden is the former orchard, which now houses the new flower garden, laid with rectangular beds and gravel paths. Very much in its infancy, it is still experiencing a few teething problems. The intention is to fill it with colour from flowering perennials (inspired in part by Herterton House, pages 124–9). A corner bed near the gate devoted to kniphofias has not so far performed to order, the kniphofias perversely blooming earlier than planned, clashing with the old-fashioned roses that sprawl over the stone walls behind. Happily, the collection of dianthus in the

The deep orange flowers, above, of Crocosmia masonorum *make a good focal point in any border (even when wind-blown, as they are here, an inevitability in a seaside garden).*

The terrace and lawns, right, in front of the house. Pots of pink geraniums and godetias, with white argyranthemums, add colour in late summer. The prominent white flower spikes are Veronicastrum virginicum album.

opposite bed has been more successful. An uncommon plant in this part of the garden is *Linaria triornithophora*, which flower-arrangers seem to go mad over. It has rose-purple snapdragon-like flowers, with brownish markings on the lower lip.

Like many gardening couples, the McBurnies have their own particular areas of interest. Growing rare and unusual plants from seed is Mr McBurnie's, and he also has a small but fascinating collection of insectivorous plants, one of them doing sterling service in the kitchen catching household flies! He collects seed from various esoteric sources including garden societies and professional overseas seed collections. His wife, who colour-plants the borders, has the job of incorporating the results into them, which can cause problems since they are often not at all sure whether the plants will turn out as described. Among the successes have been a *Fabiana imbricata*, rather like a tree heath with cream flowers, and an acaena with leaves like a silver potentilla.

In the deep borders under the shade of some large trees, the McBurnies grow a range of foliage plants, including pulmonarias, thalictrum and hostas *H. fortunei albopicta*, *H. f.* 'Albo-Marginata' and the common 'Thomas Hogg' which the slugs go for first, as well as one or two new varieties – *H.* 'Julie Morss', for example. They were particularly pleased to find a new sport of *Hosta sieboldiana* appear on a plant they received from Sunningdale nurseries many years ago, which they have registered as 'Borwick Beauty'.

Many of the island beds in the lawns are themed in various ways. There is a blue bed, with eryngiums, malva and agapanthus, and one for silver-leaved plants with artemisias, centaureas and *Calceolaria arachnoidea*, and a gold border with *Catalpa bignonioides* 'Aurea', golden privet and *Hosta* 'Gold Standard'. Despite the salt winds, the gardens have an enviable microclimate, and the McBurnies manage to grow both a passion flower and an exotic trumpet vine on the house wall.

A grass path leads to another part of the garden where the old stone walls are covered with roses, old-fashioned perennial sweet pea and clematis 'Mrs Cholmondeley'; and *Billardiera longiflora* which, in September, has large purple berries. By the gate there is a *Wisteria sinensis* and the unusual *Vestia lycioides* (*V. foetida*) with yellow fuchsia-like flowers and elongated seed pods.

Unlike so many gardens in the south, which peak in June, Bank House stays looking good until late September.

In the shady borders, right, with hydrangeas and hostas on the left and pink and white herbaceous plants on the right, including a pink hebe, Achillea *'Taygetea', the pink phlox 'Elizabeth Campbelli', the white flowers of* Romneya coulteri *and the shrub rose 'Pink Grootendorst'.*

A quiet corner of the garden, below, where a gateway leads through to the green and gold borders. Alchemilla, corydalis, ferns and ivy grow well in the light shade.

Sparkling bronze stems of Stipa gigantea, *left, provide the focal point in this part of the garden. Nearly matching them in height are spires of* Salvia sclarea turkestanica *with the fluffy flowers of* Gypsophila 'Rosy Veil' *in the foreground.*

Penn

*A predominantly woodland garden with magnolias,
rhododendrons, azaleas and camellias, set on a
steep, exposed site on Alderley Edge*

Open for more than twenty years under the National Gardens Scheme, Penn has a much-prized collection of more than five hundred rhododendrons and azaleas, as well as many different camellias and magnolias. Set on a sharp escarpment of Alderley Edge, the house was built by the Manchester architect Percy Worthington in 1912. The Baldwins have added to the garden, taking in an area of woodland at the top of the hill, where to their delight the conditions (after much hard work) turned out to be ideal for a wide range of rhododendrons.

Among the many splendid species at Penn is *R. montroseanum* (named after the Duchess of Montrose of Brodick), with its huge silvery leaves and trusses of magnificent pink flowers. Other Himalayan species include *R. falconeri eximium*, with good heads of white, purple-spotted flowers in April and remarkable suede-like foliage in June, *R. rex*, now a tree over 6 m (20 ft) high, with similar flowers and dark green, red-felted leaves, and, a particular favourite of Mr Baldwin's, *R. macabeanum*, with its apple-green, thickly cream-felted leaves and lovely heads of lemon bells in April. This small tree is draped with the blue *Clematis alpina*, and backed in June by the deliciously fragrant saucer-shaped blooms of a tall *Magnolia sinensis*.

The countless hybrid rhododendrons include the handsome primrose-yellow 'Mariloo', a *lacteum* cross raised at Exbury and named after a member of the Rothschild family, 'Polar Bear' with its huge ice-white blooms in late summer, and, of course, the most famous of all hybrids, 'Loderi' (in various forms), with enormous white, cream or pink trusses in May, all of them fragrant.

The Baldwins are equally proud of their collection of magnolias. A couple of the larger ones were already planted when they bought the house, but they themselves planted the *Magnolia stellata* nearly forty years ago, a small one with very early, pure white flowers, and a form called *M.* 'Caerhays Pink', which is often mistaken for *M. campbellii*, but is quicker to come to flower. It is a

*The handsome yew arch, above, in the
lawned area below the house provides an
ideal backdrop for the display of spring
blossom from the* Prunus kurilensis.

*The delicate pink semi-double flowers
of* Camellia 'Brigadoon' *are set off
by the surrounding evergreen foliage
frame of conifers and clipped yew.*

Several hundred *different forms of rhododendron are grown at Penn. This one,* R. glaucophyllum, *grows to about 1.4 m (5 ft), the rose-pink bell-shaped flower clusters appearing in late spring.*

hybrid between *M. sargentiana robusta* and *M. sprengeri diva*, with huge rose-purple flowers in April, which appear before the leaves. They also have another cultivar, 'Lanarth', with deeper maroon flowers, developed by Burncoose and Southdown, the magnolia specialist nursery in Redruth. Magnolias are notoriously slow to flower, but these are struck-rooted in New Zealand, and as a result they flower much earlier than the grafted magnolias, although they cost proportionately more. Other interesting ones

are 'Stardust', 'Sundew' and 'Manchu Fan', bought from Peter Smithers, who has a magnificent collection of magnolias in the hills above Lake Maggiore in Italy. Mrs Baldwin's favourite is the more common magnolia, *M. liliiflora* 'Nigra' with its deep maroon flowers over a long period from mid-spring to mid-summer. It has a particularly attractive spreading habit. Two pleasantly scented magnolias grown at Penn are *M. denudata*, with chalice-shaped flowers early in the year, and *M. hypoleuca*, the large-leaved Japanese magnolia with hanging flowers.

More than fifty different varieties of camellia also flourish at Penn, and have the advantage not only of attractive evergreen foliage, but of flowering at a much earlier age than the magnolias. Provided the soil is lime-free, they are not particularly choosy about the site, and will cope with most situations. At Penn they start flowering in January and carry on providing a spectacular display until May.

In addition, there are some fine trees at Penn, including two Californian redwoods (*Sequoia sempervirens*) – shoots struck as cuttings from a block of wood originally bought by the Baldwins in California as a table decoration. They were planted out, and against all the odds, are making startling progress, currently about 9 m (30 ft) high, with splendidly varnished trunks.

One of the less common specimens that draws visitors' attention at Penn is the Chilean fire bush (*Embothrium coccineum*), which looks quite sensational in flower, with its mass of tubular orange-red blooms. According to the Baldwins, it usually performs obediently for their open days in spring.

The woodland garden, far left, looking up the hill towards the ridge of Alderley Edge, with rhododendrons in flower in the foreground.

On the terrace, left, on the other side of the yew arch, is this splendid Magnolia × soulangeana, *seen here shortly after it has come into flower.*

Sleightholme Dale Lodge

Large country garden with a
particularly fine walled rose garden,
dating back to the turn of the century

SET ON A steep hillside in a secluded Yorkshire valley, the gardens at Sleightholme Dale Lodge incorporate a spectacular one-acre walled rose garden, created at the turn of the century by Lord Feversham, who built the Lodge as a wedding gift for his daughter, the current owner's grandmother. The gardens extend over four acres, above the house in the form of the rose garden, and below it in a series of terraces stretching down to the valley floor, where sheep graze in the meadows.

The rose garden is a remarkable combination of geometric planning and ebullient plant growth, not just in the form of the hundreds of roses but in the magnificent double border that bisects the garden vertically through its centre. Old oak frames not only support every variety of rose imaginable but screen the sections from one another, each with its own different planting character. The steep gradient on which the garden is set adds immeasurably to its charm, so that when you stand at the bottom of the double border looking up, the plants rise above you, stretching up in a glorious living tapestry of colour. The

double border is thickly planted with old-fashioned herbaceous perennials in great frothy drifts of pinks, blues, mauves and whites, with roses and clematis interwoven among them.

Within the divisions are two rectangular gardens and two circular ones, with stone paths in between. Each circle is subdivided, like the segments of a grapefruit, into eight subsections, separated by narrow stone paths. The original design concentrated solely on Hybrid Tea roses, but the current owner, Rosanna James, found that it was difficult to keep the roses in good condition after so many years in the same spot, and is now beginning to replace them with perennials and bulbs.

She has also begun to replace some of the rotting trellises, to grow some fruit and vegetables, potager-style, in one corner, and to train loganberries, blackberries, apples and redcurrants over some of the bordering trellises, in place of the roses. Although many of the original Hybrid Teas have been replaced, there are still literally hundreds of exquisite roses, in almost every form and colour. Most famous names are here from the exquisite

***Deep red** hollyhocks, above, in the walled*
garden – just one of the many old-fashioned
perennials, biennials and annuals that fill
this part of the garden in summer.

***The long double border**, right, that runs*
from top to bottom of the walled garden. Rose
borders mingle with perennials in a scheme
where tones of blue and red predominate.

*The **brilliant pink** flowers, below, in the foreground, are those of the annual mallow 'Silver Cup', while the rose almost smothering the arch is the Bourbon 'Variegata di Bologna' with double pink magenta-striped flowers.*

Centifolia 'Fantin-Latour', with its delicately sculptured double pink flowers, to the Bourbon 'Madame Pierre Oger'.

Among Mrs James's particular favourites, she picks out for special mention: *R.* 'Empress Josephine' (syn. *R. × franco-furtana*), 'Prosperity', *R. rubrifolia* (syn. *R. glauca*), 'Gypsy Boy', 'Minnehaha, 'Buff Beauty', 'Alchymist', 'Amy Robsart', *R.* 'Andrewsii', the double pink *pimpinellifolia*, *R.* 'Cantabrigiensis' and *R. chinensis* 'Mutabilis' (syn. *R. × odorata* 'Mutabilis'). They all grow, she says, in the way that is most obliging for the position they are planted in: for example, the new shoots of 'Gypsy Boy' seem to fit exactly the fence against which it is planted, while 'Minnehaha' covers an arch with flowers. 'Alchymist' never lets her down, any more than do 'Buff Beauty' and 'Prosperity'.

Beyond the high walls of the rose garden is the spring garden, an orchard with a wide variety of flowering trees, underplanted with bulbs, while the broad grassy terraces below the house are bordered with yet more roses, and a wide range of shrubs.

The view across the walled garden, far right. In summer its neat geometric divisions almost disappear under the profusion of the planting.

On the lower terraces, right, overlooking the sheep pastures, the planting changes to soft yellows, blues and greens. The poolside planting includes the giant cowslip (*Primula florindae*), *the tall bell-shaped blue flowers of* Campanula lactiflora *and the massive yellow-flowered dome of a venerable* Potentilla fruticosa, *now more than fifty years old.*

Dolwen

Cottage garden with herbaceous
perennials and woodland plants in
an idyllic setting

IF YOU persevere up a never-ending lane, deep in the hills of the Welsh marches, you eventually come across Dolwen — an ancient longhouse encircled by a fascinating cottage-style garden that, despite the singular beauty of the surroundings, never descends into chocolate-box prettiness.

Frances Denby, who has lived there for eighteen years, has gradually extended the garden from the small terrace bank in front of the house to around four acres, most of it stretching up the hillside, following the course of the stream that winds down the valley past the front garden. The stream was dug out, and the spoil used to create a bank that now rises to meet the terrace in front of the house. Here broken pieces of Welsh slate make an attractive vernacular form of alpine garden, where a wide range of plants have happily self-seeded and, by and large, have been given their head.

To one side is an informal border of mixed herbaceous plants, including *Allium bulgaricum* and *Euphorbia griffithii* 'Fireglow', and low-growing shrubs, while two standard wisterias, bought as

bonsai forms many years ago and planted out, now provide a focal point in the otherwise low-level planting. The neat hummocks of the plants in the scree bed are echoed by the contours of the clipped box hedging behind, making a more formal contrast with the unruly profusion of roses on the house walls, and a huge 'Kiftsgate' which, in Mrs Denby's words, has 'yomped' over an old apple tree and cascaded out over the lane.

To one side of the house, up the hill, a deep gulley through which the stream now flows has created an ideal habitat for shade- and moisture-loving plants like rodgersias, ligularias and ferns, many native forms of which do well in the damp Welsh climate. Just beneath an arched bridge over the gulley (its delicate form constructed, surprisingly prosaically, from bits of an old aircraft hangar) is the crouching figure of Aphrodite, which Mrs Denby commissioned from her sculptor step-daughter, Philippa Denby.

The site of the garden lies at the foot of an ancient glacier, and the residual mammoth stones now add structure and interest to

The orange-red *heads, above, of the aptly named poppy,* Papaver *'Fireball', one of many different forms grown at Dolwen.*

The front terrace, *right, with its clumps of* Euphorbia griffithii *'Fireglow', snow-in-summer and, in the background, the pink standard wisteria, one of a pair.*

the principally woodland planting higher up the hill. Here Mrs Denby houses her recent acquisitions, such as trilliums, arisaemas and phormiums. Just above it – sheltered by an arbour over which honeysuckle, jasmine and roses are being trained – a seat allows her to rest after the day's work in the garden is done and contemplate both the progress of her new charges and the long views across to the Shropshire hills.

Below this garden is a new small woodland, planted with some of Mrs Denby's favourite trees, including a young *Acer pensylvanicum* with its shocking-pink spring growth, a golden-leaved *Catalpa bignonioides* 'Aurea' and the graceful *Betula utilis jacquemontii*. Level with this area, on the other side of the lane, is a small wild woodland garden underplanted with fritillaries, bluebells and ajuga, as well as hellebores, snowdrops and Bowles' golden grass, all growing through rhododendrons and camellias.

Two large ponds on the top level were created only recently, but as yet there are no fish in them, only ducks and geese. Every day, apparently, a heron comes along to see if Mrs Denby has been foolish enough to stock the pond for him.

Around the side and the back of the house grows a wide range of old-fashioned perennials, in particular delphiniums and poppies. In this part of the garden there are some very pretty verbascums – the 'in' plant of today, although Mrs Denby herself is impervious to gardening trends, and particularly dislikes peculiarities like green flowers, twisted forms and sickly variegations. At Dolwen, she has kept her planting in keeping with the site, restraining its enthusiasm with a firm, but kindly, hand.

Aphrodite, left, crouching by the side of the stream, amid the boulders swept down the valley many thousands of years ago by a glacier.

CULTIVATION
Euphorbia

EUPHORBIAS make wonderful plants for dry, sunny borders. They range from the architectural *E. characias wulfenii*, with its massive heads of yellow-green flowers from spring onwards, to the smaller euphorbias like the bright yellow-flowered *E. cyparissias*, shown here, which also makes good ground cover.

Lower House Farm

*Plantswoman's garden on the Welsh borders,
designed to look good at all seasons, with a range
of unusual plants*

FOR MANY people, the true test of a garden is whether it can hold its form and retain its appeal as easily in autumn as in high summer. Mrs Clay at Lower House Farm has certainly succeeded in creating a garden for all seasons. When she and her husband came here in 1963 the existing planting was no inspiration, with rectangular beds in lawns, and dull lonicera hedges, but after Mrs Clay gave up horse-riding, she had time to devote to the garden. Since then, her obsession with it has grown, as she has gradually taken in more of the surrounding land to house her ever-growing plant collection.

Leading up to the house is a long drive with mature chestnuts and limes on one side (mere striplings when the Clays arrived) with a bed of contrasting green and gold foliage plants opposite, the golden tones echoed by the golden ash tree further up the drive, and the arching branches of a pyracantha, weighed down under a mass of berries. On the house walls, the colour positively blazes in autumn with the fiery red foliage of a Virginia creeper,

punctuated by the deep red blooms of a 'Dublin Bay' rose mingling with them.

Round the corner is a small paved terrace, created from York stone given to the Clays as a silver-wedding present. They laid the stone straight on to the soil, with the result that it is now a mass of sun-loving plants, including clouds of self-seeding erigeron daisies, with the scent of crushed thyme underfoot. Beyond it is a small formal area screened off by a venerable heavily fruiting apple tree, and by a pergola, covered in honeysuckle and underplanted with Mrs Clay's favourite Michaelmas daisy, *Aster × frikartii* 'Wunder von Stäffa'. Here a long, slim rectangular bed, planted simply and very effectively with *Calamintha nepeta*, culminates in a small antique statue of a horse on a plinth, the view of the countryside beyond glimpsed through the feathery branches of a large willow.

The willow was here when the Clays arrived, but has never really looked entirely happy with its lot, although it battles on each year. Mrs Clay was given some seeds of *Lathyraea clandestina*,

The curving border, *above, on the boundary echoes the contours of the countryside beyond, with the russet stems of the dogwoods providing a focal point in autumn.*

The stone greyhound, *right, seen through the striking scarlet heads of* Penstemon *'Cherry' and set off by* Berberis, *ivies and a variegated holly.*

CULTIVATION
Bupleurum fruticosum

A USEFUL evergreen shrub for the sunny border, *Bupleurum fruticosum* (below, in the foreground) has blue-green foliage and starry heads of yellow flowers, turning to bronzy seed heads as the season lengthens. *Salix elaeagnos* (behind) makes a good backcloth with yellow catkins in spring and coppery leaves in autumn.

a form of toothwort which grows as a parasite on willow and poplar. She stuck the seeds on the roots of the willow, and forgot about them. Four years later, they astonished her by coming up in force in spring – small purple-hooded flowers in tight clusters only an inch or two high – coinciding, curiously enough, with an article on them in *The Garden* magazine.

Mixed perennial and shrub borders line the lawn beyond and punctuate it at various points, screened from each other by the careful positioning of specimen plants, like the *Malus* × *robusta*, whose cherry-red fruit last till Christmas, underplanted with single white-flowered shasta daisies. The tree has been blown over flat on three separate occasions and winched back upright using a tractor. It now has a huge prop to support it, and against all the odds seems to be thriving.

Behind the house is a stream, fed by a spring higher up the garden, lined with shade- and moisture-loving plants like rodgersias, ligularia, astilbes, hostas, polygonum and cimicifuga, and a pool and enclosure for several pairs of different ornamental ducks.

At the far end of the lawn, just in front of the tennis court, is the most recently planted area of the garden, taken in from the surrounding fields a couple of years ago. Among the many plants in the borders putting on a good autumn show are a range of hardy chrysanthemums, including 'Bronze Elegance', and a pretty, soft buttery yellow sport of it, christened 'Nantyderry Sunshine', which Mrs Clay is putting in for an award.

The deep, rich reddish purple of berberis, the fiery autumn leaves of amelanchier, the great golden quince of chaenomeles, a wide range of Michaelmas daisies, *Acer rubrum* 'October Glory' (a specially selected clone for autumn colouring), and the wonderful russet leaves of a vine, *Vitis vinifera* 'Purpurea', grown over the pavilion by the swimming pool, are among the many plants that add their contribution later in the year.

The foliage, left, of Virginia creeper and the ornamental vine Vitis cognetiae *puts on a fiery autumn display. At their feet are chrysanthemums, including the bright yellow-flowered 'Jante Wells' and the softer coloured 'Cottage Apricot'.*

Brilliant red leaves and flowers, above, at the front of the house, in the form of the foliage of the Virginia creeper on the house walls and the matching flowers of the busy Lizzies at the base of the wisteria.

Blaengwrfach Isaf

*Steeply sloping cottage garden with
a stream and particularly
attractive spring planting*

F EW GARDENERS are satisfied with their achievements, and Barry and Gail Farmer are no exception. At Blaengwrfach Isaf, they have created a charming semi-wild woodland garden, which draws a rich variety of wildlife to it, in a particularly beautiful setting. According to Mrs Farmer, when she came here thirty years ago her heart was set on having a cottage garden, full of sun-loving herbaceous plants. Through enthusiasm and inexperience, she says, she planted too close and now the canopy of the trees and larger shrubs has spread in many areas of the garden to create a shady woodland. From a wildlife point of view, the garden has worked out wonderfully well. Both Barry and Gail Farmer are interested in natural history, and thanks to the varied habitat that they have introduced into the garden they now have, among others, spotted and pied flycatchers and redstarts breeding in the garden, as well as lots of rare hoverflies.

Sloping steeply down the valley to a small stream, the garden is not the easiest to work. There is very little topsoil, with the solid rock on which the garden is based showing through in places. In other areas, the land was so damp that it was once a quaking bog. They improved as best they could on nature, adding topsoil and draining the marshier areas where possible, and have now turned it to their advantage to grow either scree plants or moisture-loving plants respectively. Despite the rocky subsoil, the trees they have planted have grown with unexpected vigour to reach surprising heights in a very short space of time. The Canadian red alders bought as two-year seedlings have made an impressive amount of growth, as have the now huge willows.

The garden is open in spring, when it is at its best with the fresh young foliage of the trees, like the acers and many different forms of sorbus, including the light-catching creamy white leaves of *S. aria* 'Lutescens'. The Farmers are also continually adding to their collection of spring bulbs. For summer interest, they grow a large number of climbing roses and clematis which can scramble towards the light. They planted more than twenty-five different clematis in the garden, along with some of the large scrambling roses. Although not all the clematis have coped, when they do thrive, they make rapid progress, among them a *Clematis armandii* on the terrace and *C. spooneri* over the oak at the front of the house.

Pink and white *primulas, above, hellebores and celandine carpet the woodland floor in early spring.*

Looking down *the valley, right. Flanking the pool are* Picea abies *'Nidiformis' and* Lonicera nitida *'Baggesen's Gold'.*

Amelanchier laevis, *above, in bloom at the foot of the sloping lawn, with spring bulbs in the foreground.*

Cefn Bere

Small plantsman's garden on a
steep hillside with spectacular
views of Cader Idris

SET ON A steeply rising hillside above Dolgellau, Mr and Mrs Thomas's small garden is crammed with interesting and unusual plants, principally dwarf shrubs and alpines for which they have a special affection. Although the soil in the upper part of the garden is desperately poor and limits what can be grown, this has been turned to advantage by growing plants from the maquis, like grey sages, halimiums and cistuses.

The front garden, with its spectacular views across the valley to Cader Idris, is deliberately formal and fairly restrained. As Mr Thomas points out, there is always a clash between the view and the garden, since although the garden should ideally be enclosed, at the same time you want to be able to enjoy the long vista to the mountains beyond. To frame the view, evergreen plants that would form sculptural mounds and spread together were chosen, giving this part of the garden a strongly oriental feel. As a result it has form and structure throughout the winter, although it bursts into life in spring when the mountain rhododendrons come into flower.

On the terrace there is a collection of troughs which have been filled with alpines, including tiny rock roses, dwarf pinks, sempervivums, globularia and saxifrages. A small conifer bed to one side of the drive offers an interesting contrast in forms, with the white spruce (*Picea glauca albertiana* 'Conica'), the black spruce (*P. mariana* 'Nana') and *Juniperus communis* 'Compressa'. Their upright forms contrast with the dome shape of *Genista pilosa*, a ground-covering Mediterranean plant which in fact grows wild on Cader Idris, its most northerly limit.

Behind the house, a deep gulley and steep bank separate it from the hillside that forms the back garden. Mr Thomas uses the shade cast by the house and bank to grow a wide variety of ferns and hostas, as well as × *Gaulnettya* 'Wisley Pearl', a cross between *Gaultheria* and *Pernettya*, and an attractive evergreen shrub for shade or semi-shade, with small white flowers in summer and purplish berries all winter.

Above them is a wide range of the smaller rhododendrons, both species and hybrids, giving a great variety of flower size and colour, and perhaps even more important, of leaf and form. The

***Snakebark maple** (Acer griseum), above, is renowned for its attractive peeling orange-brown bark. It needs to be grown where this can be displayed to best advantage.*

***The front garden**, right, looking towards Cader Idris. The sculptural forms of the conifers and the rhododendrons echo the forms of the mountains on the horizon.*

CULTIVATION
Bark and stem colour

A NUMBER of trees have attractive bark, including the snakebark maple (*Acer griseum*). Other good subjects are the paper birch (*Betula papyrifera*), whose bark hangs in pinkish-bronze tatters. Some of the cherries have attractive polished-looking trunks, including the Tibetan cherry (*Prunus serrula*) the bark of which is a rich reddish brown. On a smaller scale some of the dogwoods, including *Cornus alba*, provide excellent winter stem colour. *Rubus cockburnianus* also has glistening white winter stems, and some of the willows are chiefly grown for winter stem colour, including *Salix alba* 'Britzensis' which has orange-red young shoots. Plants grown for stem colour are normally cut back almost to ground level in early spring.

Some of the many species rhododendrons and azaleas, left, which do particularly well at Cefn Bere, including R. campylogynum *and* R. kiusianum *framing a snakebark maple in the centre of the picture.*

The troughs of alpines, right, on the terrace in the front garden. Mr Thomas has a large collection of them, many of which he grows from seed.

grace and delicacy of the flowers and leaves of the wild and near-wild forms are increasingly being appreciated.

The rhododendrons are underplanted with dwarf bulbs, including snowdrops, snowflakes, erythronium, cyclamen, narcissus and allium. These give colour and interest at different times of the year without taking up precious garden space. Spring bulbs are planted with hostas, for which they are ideal companions, as they finish flowering as the hosta leaves emerge.

Among the perennials that flourish on this Welsh hillside are the blue poppy *Meconopsis × sheldonii* and clumps of *Ranunculus aconitifolius* 'Flore Pleno', fair maids of France, with button-like white flowers and deeply divided leaves. There is also a good range of old Musk roses, and Mr Thomas is fond of the garden hybrids of the Burnet roses of the dunes, *Rosa pimpinellifolia* 'Lutea Plena' (syn. *R.* 'Lutea Maxima'), 'Staffa' and 'William III'.

The hybrid × Gaulnettya *'Wisley Pearl', above, is an attractive dense shrub with small white flowers in early summer and purplish red fruits in autumn. The neat evergreen* *foliage makes a good contrast with the large green leaves of the* Hosta fortunei *in front of it. Both are good subjects for shady parts of the garden.*

Index

Index compiled by Hilary Bird

Addresses

All the gardens described in this book are privately owned, and are open in aid of the National Gardens Scheme each year on specific dates or by appointment.

Visitors are asked to check in the National Gardens Scheme publication *Gardens of England and Wales* (the Yellow Book) for details of opening dates and times.

Locations and admission charges for these gardens as well as for all the other gardens open for the Scheme (over 2,600) are given in the Yellow Book, which is published annually. It is available from booksellers at £1.50, or from the National Gardens Scheme, Hatchlands Park, East Clandon, Guildford, Surrey GU4 7RT at £2.25 incl. postage.

Bank House, Borwick, Lancashire
Bates Green Farm, Arlington, Sussex
Beth Chatto Gardens, Elmstead Market, Essex
Blaengwrfach Isaf, Bancyffordd, Dyfed
Brook Cottage, Alkerton, Oxfordshire
Cecily Hill House, Cirencester, Gloucestershire
Cefn Bere, Cae Deintur, South Gwynned
Chilcombe House, near Bridport, Dorset
Chyverton, Zelah, Cornwall
Dolwen, Cefn Coch, Powys
Elsing Hall, near Dereham, Norfolk
Field Farm, Iden Green, Kent
Fitz House, Teffont Magna, Wiltshire
17 Fulham Park Gardens, London SW6
Gardener's Cottage, West Dean, Sussex
Greencombe, Porlock, Somerset
Hazelby House, North End, Berkshire
Herterton House, Morpeth, Northumberland
Ken-Caro, Bicton, Cornwall

Lower House Farm, Nantyderry, Gwent
Magnolia House, Yoxford, Suffolk
Manor House, The, Chaldon Herring, Dorset
Milton Lodge, Wells, Somerset
Old Rectory, The, Sudborough, Northamptonshire
40 Osler Road, Headington, Oxfordshire
Owl Cottage, Mottistone, Isle of Wight
Park Farm, Great Waltham, Essex
Pear Tree House, Litton, Avon
Penn, Alderley Edge, Cheshire
Putsborough Manor, near Croyde, Devon
Sleightholme Dale Lodge, Fadmoor, Yorkshire
Sticky Wicket, Buckland Newton, Dorset
Turn End, Haddenham, Buckinghamshire
Upper Mill Cottage, Loose, Kent
Vale End, Albury, Surrey
White Windows, Longparish, Hampshire
Wyken Hall, Stanton, Suffolk